If we love one another, God lives in us and
his love is made complete in us.

—1 JOHN 4:12 (NIV)

SECRETS *From* GRANDMA'S ATTIC

SECRETS From GRANDMA'S ATTIC

Turn Back the Dial

Roseanna M. White

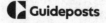
Guideposts

Published by Guideposts
100 Reserve Road, Suite E200
Danbury, CT 06810
Guideposts.org

Cover and interior design by Müllerhaus
Cover illustration by Greg Copeland at Illustration Online LLC.
Typeset by Aptara, Inc.

ISBN 978-1-961126-00-8 (hardcover)
ISBN 978-1-961126-01-5 (epub)

Printed and bound in the United States of America
10 9 8 7 6 5 4 3 2 1

Turn Back the Dial

Chapter One

Tracy Doyle waved to Jana, Matt, Colton, and Natalie with a wide smile, sending a wink over their heads at Amy and Miles. She'd been hoping that February would give her—and all of them, really—time to rest and recuperate after the frantic packing and moving and wedding prep, but thus far she still felt pretty exhausted. Even so, she'd volunteered to watch the four kids for the day while Amy and Miles ran some errands and tackled some unpacking that hadn't yet been done.

"Thanks again!" her sister called from the sidewalk as she herded the children toward the car.

Tracy gave one more wave and folded her arms across her sweater to hold in what warmth was to be found on this chilly Saturday. "Anytime," she called back. And she meant it. Even if she did then slip into the house, close the winter out with a shiver, and breathe a happy, tired sigh.

She didn't regret for a moment helping Amy with the flurry of packing or planning when she and Matt and Jana had to vacate their house so quickly. She enjoyed the week the three of them had stayed at her house before the wedding, and had been the first to volunteer to help move their stuff into the Anderson house.

But boy, some of her muscles still ached from the effort, and the thought of hibernating through the rest of winter sounded pretty good right about now.

Of course, if she meant to hibernate, she better have a snack first. She smiled as she breathed in the fragrance of the cookies she'd had Natalie and Jana help her make that morning. The boys had been out in the garage with her husband, Jeff, most of the day, helping him with a shelf he was building, but the girls had both declined. That, she'd decided, was the perfect excuse for breaking out the recipe for the double-chocolate chewy cookies she'd spotted on the internet the week before. Now she breathed in a deep, chocolaty breath and was glad they'd made a double batch. She'd sent most of them home with Amy's crew but still had plenty to enjoy.

She nabbed one now, along with the dregs from the morning's pot of coffee. After popping that into the microwave for a minute, she took cup and cookie into the living room, sank onto the couch with another sigh that made her aware of every one of her years, and bit into the cookie.

Her eyes slid closed as the flavors melted on her tongue. The last few weeks had been nonstop. Ultimately happy but also chaotic. Her heart felt full to the brim as she considered the contentment on her sister's face a few minutes ago when she and Miles had stepped into the kitchen and called for their kids—*theirs*, together. There had already been a few bumps as everyone adjusted to the idea of their new family, and there would be things to sort out yet in terms of details and the realities of six people living together in a house that had previously had only three.

But it would be good. It would be beautiful.

God had created something new.

She must have dozed off for a few minutes after finishing her coffee because she jerked to attention when the door shut, pushing herself up from where she'd somehow ended up cuddled with a throw pillow, Sadie asleep on the floor beside her. Or maybe more than a few minutes. A glance at the clock told her that an hour and a half had slipped by. And the winter sun had gone into hiding while she slumbered the afternoon away.

Whoops. She'd meant to start dinner after she enjoyed her coffee and cookie, not take a nap. Looked like leftovers might be the order of business instead of the chicken and pasta dish she'd been planning.

She stood and followed the sounds of running water to the kitchen, where Jeff was scrubbing his hands at the sink. He tossed a smile at her over his shoulder. "You look like you just had a nice nap."

"Mm?" She lifted a hand to her cheek and felt the dent from the throw pillow there. No doubt her hair was flattened on that side too. Chuckling, she shrugged. "What can I say? It may take me months to recover from January."

Jeff laughed too. "We're not kids anymore, that's for sure. Moving felt a whole lot easier a few years ago. You know what I think we need?"

Leaning a hip against the counter, Tracy made a show of considering. "Pizza? Chinese food? Tacos?"

The tilt of his head said all those options had their merits. "I could be convinced. But I was thinking something bigger. Like a vacation."

"A vacation." She repeated the phrase with a little sigh, this one longing. "That sounds nice." Though with the spring semester underway, that certainly would have to wait. No way would Jeff take a whole week off before spring break. But planning something for then could be entertaining, even refreshing. "Someplace warm, maybe?"

"Maybe." But he didn't say it like he was dreaming of palm trees and white sand beaches. He said it like he had something up his sleeve already.

Tracy straightened again and narrowed her eyes. "What are you planning, Jeffrey Doyle?" Something for their anniversary, perhaps, on Valentine's Day? Though it wasn't like thirty-two years was a typical milestone.

His grin was boyish. "Tell you what. I'll go pick up some dinner for us, and then we can listen to *Turn Back the Dial*, and I'll tell you what I'm thinking."

A frown weighed down Tracy's brows. They'd listened to the twin radio programs broadcast on Saturday nights from Culver-Stockton a few times before—*Jukebox Saturday Night*, which played big band music, and then *Turn Back the Dial*, which aired old radio shows. Dramas, comedies, mysteries. They were entertaining, but they weren't part of their routine by any stretch of the imagination, and they usually listened to them on a whim. They didn't *plan* it.

Clearly Jeff knew something she didn't. "Um...okay."

He toweled his hands dry, still smiling. "I ran into Ken Frost on campus yesterday," he said of the shows' host. "He said they had something fun planned and gave me a little hint of what it was. I promised him we'd tune in. So, takeout?"

Apparently, he wanted her to discover this "something fun" during the broadcast rather than telling her about it now. Well, she could play along with that, especially if it meant getting something for dinner other than the spaghetti in the fridge that she'd already had twice this week. They debated the merits of the various takeout places nearby for a few minutes before deciding on enchiladas. Tracy called in the order at Los Nopales, and Jeff grabbed his keys.

Ordinarily she would have offered to ride along with him, but the kitchen still bore the marks of the cookie baking, so she opted for staying behind and doing some cleanup while he fetched the food.

She went ahead and switched on the aging radio, tuning it to the college's station just in time to hear the music program's adopted theme song, "Jukebox Saturday Night," performed by Glenn Miller and the Modernaires.

While big band music wasn't her daily go-to, she always enjoyed it when it was on. Tonight, it put a swing in her step while she did the dishes, put them and the cookies away, and side-stepped Sadie, who had, of course, plopped herself down in the middle of the floor so she could watch Tracy's every dancing move.

She was filling water glasses when Jeff returned with paper bags in hand. He pulled out chips and salsa and two boxes with enchiladas, Spanish rice, and refried beans that smelled fabulous even before he took the lids off.

"Oh, this was a good idea," she said as she sat, her hand stretched toward Jeff's.

He took her fingers, grinned, and said the blessing.

Tracy had just lifted her first bite to her lips when Ken's convivial voice came on the radio between songs. "And that was tonight's 'Let's Let Bing Sing' selection. Now, as we're bebopping our way to Valentine's Day, I want to remind all of our lovely listeners about our annual Swingin' Gala. This year it'll be held at the old hotel ballroom on the weekend after Valentine's Day, and do we have a treat for you! No, not just live music by Harmony Corner, though that will be a delight. But there will also be a grand announcement of the winner of a contest that I'll give you all the details for in the next hour. So stay tuned through the rest of *Jukebox Saturday Night* and into *Turn Back the Dial*, friends, because you don't want to miss out on this one."

"A contest, huh?" Tracy forked up some rice and sent her husband a probing look. "What kind of contest? Something we'll be good at?"

Jeff laughed around his bite of enchilada, answering only after he'd swallowed. "Oh, honey. This one is right up your alley."

And it had something to do with a vacation, given his initial bringing up of the subject. Interesting, indeed. What sort of contest would have a vacation as a prize?

It was no doubt something small. A weekend at a local B and B or something. She'd never heard of the college's tiny community station doing anything all that grand. It received most of its funding, after all, through grants and donations.

Even so, Jeff's secrecy and grins made her think it would be something fun. Entertaining. And the prize must be desirable if he'd mentioned it like he had.

She probably shouldn't let those visions of palm trees keep swaying in her imagination, but… With a salute of her fork, she acknowledged the promise of the contest. "You're not going to tell me anything about it?"

"Ken will tell you soon enough." Jeff scooped some salsa onto a chip, eyes twinkling. "Besides, I don't know the details. Only the gist."

"Fine, fine. Then you'd better distract me. How were Matt and Colton on the latest restoration project?"

Jeff regaled her with tales of the boys' enthusiasm for learning to use a drill and of how carefully Matt had applied the stain to the shelf he was working on. She shared what fun the girls had enjoyed in the kitchen, offering a sample for their dessert. They finished up, put everything away, loaded the dishwasher, and were taking their cookies and glasses of milk into the living room when the hour changed, and the radio program changed with it.

Tracy listened as the intro for *Turn Back the Dial* came on. Honestly, even when they tuned in for the music, she rarely kept it on for the radio show afterward. Listening to the hour's rebroadcast of an old scripted program required too much focused attention, unlike music that could just play in the background while she did something else. Though there had been a couple over the years that she'd enjoyed listening to.

The canned intro faded out, and Ken's voice came over the airwaves again. "Hello, hello, guys and dolls. I hope you're all having a swingin' good Saturday night. Tonight on *Turn Back the Dial*, we're going to be listening to one of the highest-rated shows across the airwaves in 1948—*Windy City Gumshoes*, starring Heath Reynolds and Betty Gardiner as investigative team Joe and Josie, sibling mystery-solvers."

A mystery show. Those tended to have a plot unto themselves that didn't require foreknowledge of the rest of the series. That was nice. A couple of times she'd heard the start of a drama and turned it off simply because she had no idea who anyone was. Tracy dipped her cookie into her milk and then hurried it to her mouth before it could break.

Jeff had already polished off his first cookie, and rather than reach for his second, he instead grabbed a notebook and pen, uncapping the second with a flourish.

Interesting. This would require note-taking. Tracy took a sip of milk and gave Ken's voice her undivided attention.

"*Windy City Gumshoes* came across the airwaves every Friday night at eight from 1946 to 1949, reaching nationwide syndication by the time it went off the air at the end of the decade. And that, guys and gals, is a mystery in and of itself. A mystery *you* are invited to solve."

Jeff had written down the name of the show and of the two starring voice actors, along with the dates.

"In February 1949, the show simply went off the air at the height of its popularity, when its lead voice actor, Heath Reynolds, vanished. What happened to Heath? Why didn't the show continue, bringing in a new actor? Why did all mention of both the actor and the show vanish so quickly from the headlines? Why did the show leave its audience hanging in the middle of a five-part series? These are the questions you're going to answer."

Tracy pursed her lips as Jeff scribbled that information down.

Ken continued. "These final episodes, as they turned out to be, were in fact unique. Rather than being recorded in-studio as usual, in a grand publicity stunt, the show hit the road, traveling the very path that the characters took, as they were taking it, week by week. The cast and crew left Chicago and recorded each week's episode in the studio of a local radio station in the town in which the next one was set."

Tracy reached for her phone, pulled up a map, and dropped a pin in Chicago.

"In the show, the sleuths were engaged in a multi-episode mystery, chasing clues from Chicago south to Indianapolis, then cutting west to Peoria and—you guessed it, my friends—right here to Canton, Missouri. Rumor had it that the show and its cast were supposed to end up in Kansas City for the big finale, but they never made it there. The episode recorded here in 1949 was the last one ever to reach the airwaves."

Tracy dropped pins in the locations, tracing the route south and then west. The indirect path would have made for a long day but an easy month, if they only traveled once a week to the next stop.

"All along the way, the stars of the show were met with crowds of enthusiastic fans eager to get a glimpse of the faces that belonged to their favorite voices. And all across America, at-home sleuths tried to put together the same clues as the actors to solve the mystery of the missing coffee heiress…only to end up with the mystery of the missing radio show star."

And if the stars were last seen in Canton, then it could be reasonably surmised that there had been clues to be found here.

Then, anyway. In 1949. But now, seventy-five years later?

"Back in 1949, an investigation was launched, but an answer was never found. An answer there is, though, my friends, and a winner will be drawn from everyone who sends the correct solution to me at Ken at Turn Back the Dial dot com. The winner will win—are you ready for this?—an all-expenses-paid Mississippi River cruise for two to New Orleans! This romantic getaway will be presented to the winning couple at our annual Swingin' Gala at the old hotel ballroom, the Saturday after Valentine's Day. That's only two weeks from now, friends. So get your sleuthing caps out!"

A river cruise? Tracy had always thought one of those would be fun, and she'd been wanting to go to New Orleans for years. She looked over to Jeff and found him smiling at her. Obviously, he knew that. That was why he'd been excited for her to learn about the contest and its prize.

On the radio, Ken launched a bit of celebratory music, giving Tracy the chance to say, "This sounds like fun!" without the fear of missing any details.

"Doesn't it? I bet you can unearth all the old investigation findings in the newspaper's archives, so we'll at least know as much as they did then."

Absolutely. No doubt others in town could learn the same using the library's microfiche collection, but she loved going through the actual archives. And if Ken could promise that the answers existed and he would know the right solution when it came into his inbox, then obviously the clues were there. Someone had found them before now.

"Can't be anything too dire and grisly, right?" Jeff said with a chuckle. "They wouldn't be celebrating a cold-case murder with a river cruise."

"Yeah, that wouldn't scream 'romantic getaway.'"

The music faded out again, Ken's voice taking over. "We'll play one episode a night and cycle through all four, in order, from now until the gala, so if you miss one the first time, you can catch it again four days later. Are there clues in the episodes? That's for me to know and you to find out. But take care with your answers, friends. You can only turn in *one* solution to these questions: What happened to Heath Reynolds? Why did *Windy City Gumshoes* go off the air? And lastly, why was it forgotten? Are you ready? Here's the show."

More music played, this time with a voice-over that gave the tagline of the show. *In the windy city, mysteries abound, but none whose answer can't be found by this intrepid duo, lovely Josie and her big brother, Joe...*

Music again, and then the sound of footsteps and a squeaking, creaking door. Tracy pulled up a note app on her phone while Jeff drew a line on his paper and wrote *Episode 1* under it. They shared a smile.

Hers grew when Jeff flipped a few pages and showed her what was hidden in the back of his notebook. Two tickets to the Swingin' Gala. He must have purchased them at the college yesterday.

Well. Even if they didn't solve the mystery, they were going to have a fun Valentine weekend. And a mystery to solve would keep the two weeks until then interesting too.

Chapter Two

Though she'd managed to stay focused on the sermon and worship service while it was going on, the moment Pastor Gary said the benediction, Tracy found her thoughts turning to the radio show mystery.

She and Jeff had both taken notes as they listened to the episode of *Windy City Gumshoes* last night, laughing afterward at how they noted entirely different things. Ken had come back on at the end to announce that the next episode would be aired at six on Sunday evening, so they were already planning to listen again tonight, even though it would mean corralling the whole family to listen too, during their weekly dinner. She'd wanted to do some initial research online last night, but her daughter, Sara, had called, and they'd ended up chatting for an hour. After that, Tracy had been ready for bed.

Her dreams, though, had been full of sepia-toned private investigators, lots of exaggerated sound effects, and a maze in downtown Canton that she walked over and over. She was looking forward to diving into research on this mystery after lunch, that was for sure.

Her ears tuned in to the conversations around her, listening for keywords in other conversations. Surely everyone would be talking about the contest, right? With a river cruise as a prize, it was guaranteed to be popular.

"Looks like we've got a cold snap coming in later this week," someone said from behind her.

"Have you tried that new restaurant in Quincy yet?" This from two pews in front of her.

"We're going to take the kids to that trampoline park next weekend. Pray no one breaks an arm."

Tracy pursed her lips. Or maybe she and Jeff had a pretty good chance. Maybe there would be only a handful of people around town looking for the answer to the mystery.

"Hey." Amy appeared at her side, Bible in hand and gaze scouring the back of the sanctuary, no doubt tracking a kid or four. "I need that cookie recipe you made with the girls yesterday. Those things are to die for."

Tracy gathered her own Bible and coat. "I'll send it to you."

"The kids had a great time yesterday. They were talking all evening about the carpentry and the baking."

"Oh, good. The girls told me all about how much they're enjoying sharing a room. Though I daresay they'll have moments when they *don't* love it so much too." Tracy winked. "You can bet that we'll be praying for you guys as you settle in. I know last month wasn't all smooth sailing."

"Ha!" Amy smiled, despite the panic she'd had before the wedding when all her reservations were mysteriously canceled. It had turned out beautifully anyway. "Prayers appreciated. Now." Her sister lifted her brows. "What are you up to? You were over here scoping out the congregation like you were trying to figure out who took the last cup of coffee from the pot and didn't start another."

Though she wanted to defend herself, Tracy had to laugh. An empty coffeepot had indeed caused a bit of huffing a time or two when people were denied their caffeine. And she might have been listening a little too intently to other people's conversations. "I guess I had my competitive streak on. Have you heard about the *Turn Back the Dial* contest?"

Amy blinked. And blinked again. "The what now?"

Not a surprise that her sister hadn't turned the radio to 91.9 last night. Did Amy even have a radio in her house? Tracy quickly brought her up to speed, expecting the familiar light of challenge to fill her eyes. And it sparked, glimmered…but then banked. "That sounds fun," she said once Tracy had finished the explanation, "but Miles and I won't be entering. Settling in at home with the kids is the only thing on our agenda for the immediate future. But if you need help for your own entry, I can google with the best of them."

Tracy smiled. "I'm sure I'll take you up on that. Not to mention that the next episode will air during dinner tonight, so you'll all be forced to listen anyway."

"I won't complain about the entertainment—it does sound interesting. I bet Robin will have more time to help with it. Or maybe she'll want to enter, I guess."

Tracy laughed again. "Don't you remember the one and only time she and Terry tried something on a boat? He spent the whole weekend either at the rails or unconscious from the antinausea meds. Somehow I don't think this prize will appeal to them."

Amy granted that with a tilt of her head. "Ah, right. That was so long ago, I didn't even remember. Well then, she's a perfect sleuthing buddy for this."

Tracy nodded over Amy's shoulder at Miles making his way up the center aisle toward them. "Looks like you're being hunted down, Mrs. Anderson." She grinned at the way her sister blushed at the new name. Then she directed her smile at her new brother-in-law. "Morning, Miles."

"Morning, Tracy." He slipped an arm around Amy, contentment practically seeping from him. "Have big plans for the week?"

"Of course she does. She's going to solve a seventy-five-year-old mystery and win a free vacation. Probably before going to bed tonight." Amy winked at her.

Tracy slipped her arms into the sleeves of her coat. The heater always kicked off at noon, and she could feel its loss within a minute or two. "Right. I'm just that good."

"I wouldn't bet against you. Especially if the two of you pair up. And if you get Robin involved, watch out, world." Miles gave Amy a squeeze. "Is this the radio thing? Jeff mentioned it."

"Yep. Had you heard about it otherwise?" Tracy found herself looking around to see if anyone was listening and then laughed at herself. Sure, their chances were better if fewer people entered, but it wasn't as though the contest was a secret. And she certainly didn't have any information yet that needed protecting.

Their friends and neighbors were milling about, involved in their own conversations.

Miles shook his head. "I doubt you'll have much competition. I've looked into the local stations for ads and community calendar announcements, and that station doesn't have a huge listenership."

"Really?" Perhaps it shouldn't have surprised her. They did some syndicated news shows and classical music during the day and an assortment of obscure musical history features in the evenings. Not exactly what most people she knew listened to daily, herself included. Though she appreciated it and was glad it was there when it *was* what she wanted. "I guess it isn't really chasing any trends."

"No, but from what their press material claims, their audience is devoted." Miles shrugged. "So maybe I'm wrong. You could well be competing with every single big band fan in the county."

That could be an entertaining assortment of people. It would be interesting to see if she and Jeff ran into any other amateur sleuths chasing down clues as they blazed a trail of their own. Tracy pulled her hair out from beneath her collar. "We'll just assume there's stiff competition and solve the mystery at record-breaking speed."

The kids came charging up the aisle, darting around slow-moving adults and then flocking around Amy and Miles with four-toned chatter that seemed to have something to do with grilled cheese and tomato soup and a movie waiting for them at home.

Tracy waved them on. "That sounds like a lovely plan for the afternoon. Enjoy, everyone. And I'll see you all for supper."

Jana and Natalie slipped into the pew to give Tracy a hug, then each grabbed a parent's hand and started tugging.

Amy laughed and said over her shoulder. "See you at dinner!"

"Bye." She turned to search for Jeff and saw him chatting with some guys a few pews up. The knot of them was untangling even as she debated who else to say hello to, so she waited for Jeff to return to her side. They greeted a few more friends as they made their way out the door, gave the obligatory shiver upon stepping into the chilly air, and hurried toward their car.

The kids had the right idea with the grilled cheese and tomato soup lunch plan. The air had that damp cold to it that got into her bones, and the wind had picked up overnight, making it feel far colder than the thermometer claimed. She'd be glad to get into her nice warm house and change into something comfy and cozy.

"All well with the Andersons?" Jeff asked once he'd backed out of their parking spot.

"They seemed in good spirits. Apparently, they have big plans for grilled cheese, tomato soup, and streaming a movie this afternoon."

"Sounds pretty perfect on a day like today." Jeff cast a dubious look toward the sky. It was gray and overcast, like it was half the winter. There was no precipitation in the forecast this week, at least. But there was a cold snap moving in, which promised to drop the temperatures down into the teens and twenties. It made Tracy cold just thinking about it.

"I agree. Any movie we want to watch before we have to start dinner prep?"

"I don't know, but that gives me an idea. Think we can find episodes of *Windy City Gumshoes* in an online archive somewhere?"

"That's a good question." She was tempted to pull out her cell phone and start searching now, but they'd be home in a few minutes, and it would be easier to do it on her computer. "We can look after lunch. And see what we can dig up in general on the show."

"My thoughts exactly."

When they pulled into their driveway, Tracy had a sudden memory of running up to it one winter when she was a girl. There'd been snow, and the house had looked like a picture postcard. She'd burst through the doors, and the scents of soup and fresh bread had been in the air, and she remembered marveling at how perfect it all seemed. Back when the cold never bothered her and she didn't care if the sidewalks needed shoveling.

She smiled at the memory. "I wonder what radio shows Grandma and Grandpa listened to in 1949." They'd have been married a few years by then, the parents of young children. Did they find the time to tune in to favorite programs in the evenings? She didn't recall them ever mentioning any, even though they hadn't had a television for their first decade of married life. They'd told the story many a time about getting their first set on their tenth anniversary in 1955. Something else would have provided their entertainment before that, and radio was likely. "Kind of funny, isn't it? To think of how we've nearly forgotten about that era?"

"It is, in a way. But it also makes sense, historically speaking. Radio didn't really come into its own as a form of entertainment until the twenties, and then television displaced it rather spectacularly thirty years later. That's not all that long for something to shine. I mean, we still have it today, of course, for music and sports and news. But not in the same way."

Very true. Still, it was a little sad to think of something being such a crucial part of families' lives for decades and then being pushed aside and relegated to distant, faded memories. How many people didn't even have a radio in their home anymore?

"As for your grandparents—they certainly liked mystery shows on television. It would be reasonable to think they liked the same in radio form, wouldn't it?"

"I guess. I wonder if they ever listened to *Turn Back the Dial*?" Tracy unbuckled her seat belt and climbed out of the car. When they got inside, Sadie greeted them with a wagging tail and the kitchen enveloped them with a warmth that was welcome.

They let Sadie out, changed into comfortable clothes, fixed their soup and sandwiches, and then, after they'd eaten, pulled out their laptops and began searching for whatever they could find on *Windy City Gumshoes*, the two main actors, and where they could listen to the show.

"I'm not finding much of anything," Jeff said ten minutes into his search. He'd given himself the task of looking for the episodes while Tracy researched the show in general. "There are a couple snippets on YouTube with an old poster as a still for the video, but not any complete episodes."

"I've found a few articles that describe the premise and an episode list." She scrolled down the page of that, lips pursed as she read them. They all bore the traditional "The Case of…" sort of title, which wasn't surprising. "Looks like they did a few other serial episodes over the years, but never more than two parts. This four-part one was something new, something big."

"Probably quite a publicity draw, especially if they competed with any of the daily shows that relied on continuity." When Tracy glanced over, she saw he had an image search up, showing various posters and drawings and what looked like magazine features.

Most of them were stylized, drawn in bold colors, with the male and female leads depicted as standing back-to-back. The brother with a fedora tilted down, the sister with a fascinator over well-coiffed hair. None of the images seemed to be photographic—or if they were, they were colorized in such a way that made them look drawn, regardless.

"Hmm. That doesn't really give us a glimpse of the actors, does it?" Tracy leaned closer to better see his screen as he scrolled. There were a few that showed the face of the sister character—Betty Gardiner—as she looked over her shoulder at her brother. She was either very pretty or the artists who drew the images decided to make her that way.

Of course they would. The artists would make Joe and Josie look like the *characters* rather than the actors. That was what they could do on radio shows, just like present-day artists did with animated shows. Or, for that matter, for the few scripted radio shows still on the air.

It did make her curious though. She opened a new tab and typed in *Heath Reynolds and Betty Gardiner* and then clicked to see the images.

Her brows drew together. Most of the results were for the same posters Jeff had up, though there were a couple of black-and-white photos too. The curious thing was that while the woman was clearly the same in all of them—a thirtysomething blond with styled waves in her shoulder-length hair, lips painted in that perfect Golden Age of Hollywood bow, and a smooth complexion—there were several different men at her side.

Maybe that shouldn't be surprising. Internet searches were notorious for casting a wider net than just the words one typed in, after all. She clicked on a few, fully expecting the captions to be *Betty Gardiner and*…and then list other names she'd never heard of.

The first one said *Betty Gardiner and husband Bill Gardiner*. Okay, that made sense. The second, *Betty Gardiner and costar Heath Reynolds*. Tracy made a point of studying that masculine face.

This was the man who'd vanished. Whose disappearance spelled the end of the show. This was the face of the mystery they had to solve.

He seemed to be about forty in the photo. One of those men who came off as pleasant to look at without being overly handsome, whose face had character. Ears a bit too big, a prominent nose with a strong jaw to offset it, and a wide smile.

Out of curiosity, she clicked on the next photo of Betty. This one also said *Betty Gardiner and costar Heath Reynolds*. But this was definitely not the same man as the one in the previous image. This man's ears weren't noteworthy at all, and he had a long face and a crooked—also endearing—smile. Just as everyday-handsome as the first, but different. Definitely different. He too looked like a nice guy, if one could judge such things by a photograph.

But they didn't look even a little bit alike, aside from both being male and having dark hair.

"Interesting." She opened a separate tab and typed in *Heath Reynolds*. Pausing for a moment to consider, she added *radio* and then hit Enter. She clicked on a few of the top images, opening them in new tabs. Both of the men who'd been posing with Betty were pictured...and both were listed as *Heath Reynolds, vocal actor*.

"Okay. Somebody's clearly got their wires crossed on this one." She selected one of the articles.

Heath Reynolds was born in Chicago, Illinois, in 1910 and grew up there. A brief stint in the armed services left him injured during the war and sent home with an honorable discharge. He then moved into journalism before making his radio debut as an announcer for the Guy Henry Orchestra Hour. *When the orchestra broke up in 1946, Reynolds signed on as the lead actor for a weekly mystery radio show,* Windy City Gumshoes, *which surprised the producers by becoming wildly popular despite having two unknowns as the leads. The show enjoyed great success until Reynolds's mysterious disappearance in early 1949, after which it vanished from the air. Reynolds was not married and had no children.*

She clicked on the article that accompanied the other man's picture. It was almost word for word the same biography.

That was it. A few sentences to sum up a life that ended with so many questions.

"Looks like we're going to need the clues from those last episodes of the show." Tracy drew in a long breath and reached for her milk. Not that she'd expected to solve the mystery with a ten-minute internet search. If that was possible, it wouldn't be much of a contest. But she certainly hadn't expected her first search to present more questions than answers—like why history had attached two different photos to the same biography.

"I have an idea." Jeff set his computer on the coffee table, jumped up, and dashed out of the living room. Tracy had no idea where he was going, especially when she heard the kitchen door open and close.

She put her laptop aside and gathered their napkins and glasses to take to the kitchen. By the time she'd thrown away the napkins and rinsed the glasses, Jeff was jogging back up onto the porch.

She opened the door for him—silly man hadn't even paused for a coat and shoes, though at least he wore slippers—and frowned at the old boom box in his hands. It was the ancient radio and CD player he'd been using in the garage since the '90s. More than once she'd joked about how it seemed poised to outlive all of them despite the speckles of paint on its molded black plastic and the fact that the top of its antenna had broken off circa 2001. "And you had to bring that filthy thing in here why?"

Grinning, he tapped the front of the box. It took her a second to realize he was indicating the door to the tape deck. Gracious, she hadn't even listened to a cassette tape in...decades. Plural. But when he pressed the eject button, the door popped open and revealed an old cassette with a faded label. *Fun mix*, written in Jeff's hand.

Her lips twitched into a smile. She remembered that mix—some of his favorite songs from the '80s and '90s, stolen directly from the local radio station while they aired. "You *do* realize we can just record the shows on the radio app on our phones, right?"

He sent her a long blink. "Come on, that's no fun at all. Where's the nostalgia in that?" He flashed another cassette she hadn't noticed him holding. "Not that I'm going to tape over my *fun*, of course." He winked, moved farther into the kitchen, and set the boom box on the table. "I still had a box of blanks on the shelf."

On another day, she might have asked him why he'd kept a box of blank cassettes all this time, when he hadn't actually recorded anything onto one in thirty years. Today, she wasn't going to argue about the nostalgia.

"Okay. Well, let's go do what reading we can. And then later, we'll pretend we're twenty-five again and tape our favorite radio show. You remember how to use that thing?"

He sent her an exaggerated "Oh, please" look and slid the blank tape onto the table. "You can record on your phone, you modern girl, you. I've got this covered."

"I'm totally in." Robin's eyes gleamed as she set the large salad bowl on the table, her smile wide. "This is right up my vintage alley. We'll find the answer."

Tracy grinned. "I was hoping you'd say that. For some reason Amy seems to think she won't have the bandwidth this month." This she delivered with a wink for her sister, who was setting flatware beside the plates Tracy was putting down.

Amy's smile wasn't apologetic. "I'm playing the newlywed card on this one. There are a few other things occupying my time. But I think *you* deserve to win that cruise, Tracy."

Terry had followed them in, carrying several bottles of salad dressing. He made a face. "You sure do—you and Jeff both. I'll keep my feet on dry ground, thank you very much."

Robin chuckled, but she didn't actually look upset at the thought of not vying for the prize. "And it's so fun that the contest is over your anniversary, even if you wouldn't claim the prize until summer. Just seems perfect."

A chorus of happy shrieks sounded from the living room, where Jeff entertained their grandkids. Tracy smiled at the sound as they finished setting the table. Trying to solve a mystery with Jeff was great, but it would be even more fun with the others involved.

A few minutes before six, they had the food on the table, had corralled all the family members to their seats, and Jeff had started the recording on his ancient tape deck in the kitchen. Tracy had the station cued up in her smart phone app, her phone positioned so they'd be able to hear it during the meal.

Her heart swelled a bit as she reached for the hands on either side of her. The prize was a great vacation, but even if they didn't win, the thought of being on the hunt for clues and answers with her family…that was far more exciting than a river cruise could be.

Chapter Three

Pearl hummed the last stanza of the song that had been in her head all day, making it a little slower than it would have been if the Benny Goodman Orchestra was playing it. The perfect match to the tempo of her rocking, slow enough to lull Abigail to sleep in her arms. It was getting harder and harder to fit either of the girls on her lap as her stomach grew, but Abigail didn't seem to mind the fact that her little brother or sister was kicking up a storm. Her eyes were getting heavy, her thumb firmly in her mouth.

"One more story, Daddy. One more!" On the other side of the room, Ruth bounced a little on her knees on her bed and reached for the stack of children's books.

Howard chuckled and scooped her up before she could grab another book. "You've already had me read 'one more' three times, Ruthie girl." He peppered her head with kisses and settled her against her pillow. "It's time for bed."

"But I not tired." Ruth pronounced it with enough energy to be convincing, but Pearl had to bury a smile in Abigail's downy head. Their firstborn could go from running around like a crazy little thing to being dead to the world in the matter of a minute. Only rarely did she have trouble falling asleep these days, even when Abigail was fussy.

Pearl stood, the slumbering one-year-old in her arms, and moved to the crib. As per their usual nightly routine, she rocked while Howard read, then she put Abigail down while he tucked Ruth in. She would then give their older daughter her goodnight kisses and hugs.

Over the last few months, that routine had worked like a charm for settling both girls, but who knew what it would look like a few months from now, when baby number three joined them?

She smoothed a hand over Abigail's head, smiling at the way her lips moved though her eyes didn't flutter open. Good. Pearl straightened, pressing a hand to the ache in the small of her back. She didn't even realize she'd done it until she saw the look of concern Howard sent her. She waved that away with a smile, silently assuring him she was fine.

She was. Just tired, which had been the case more often than not during this pregnancy. Someday she'd love to know how each baby could affect her body so differently. She was convinced this one was going to be a great athlete. He was always moving and rolling and performing all sorts of acrobatics. Not that she knew he was the proper term, but that was her guess this time, based on nothing but instinct and the well-knowing eyes of all the ladies at church, who swore up and down that when a woman carried a baby like that, it was a boy.

Of course, they'd said the same thing about Ruth, and they'd been wrong. Could be this time too, though she hoped not. Howard was great with the girls, but she knew he'd like to add a son to the mix. So would she. A little variety.

She crossed over to Ruth's bed as Howard tucked the blankets around her so tightly she giggled and squirmed out, just like she always did. Pearl smiled to watch them, standing out of the way when Howard gave Ruth one last kiss and then told her good night. He winked at Pearl on his way out the door.

She grinned back and then moved to sit on the side of Ruth's bed. "Good night, my precious girl." She smoothed the blankets over the toddler, even though she knew Ruth would kick them all off within an hour. When she leaned down to give her a kiss, Ruth clapped her hands to Pearl's cheeks to hold her there, an inch from her face.

"Mama, when will baby come? Tonight?"

She'd been asking that every night for weeks. Pearl chuckled and covered Ruth's tiny little hands with her own. "No sweetie, not tonight. Three more months."

And, as she had every night for weeks, Ruth got a puzzled look on her face. How to explain a month to a child not yet three years old? She held Ruth's fingers in her own, thinking about it for a moment. "Do you remember Thanksgiving?" At Ruth's nod, Pearl said, "The time between Thanksgiving and now is about the same as the time between now and when the baby will come." Close enough, anyway.

Ruth's eyes lit up. "Christmas again!"

Okay, perhaps that wasn't the best way to measure the time. "No, sweetie," she said, trying not to either laugh or wince at the thought. "Christmas won't come again right now—but Easter will. The baby should come just a little while after Easter."

"Bunnies!"

"That's right." She nearly checked her watch but didn't let herself. Tired as she was, Pearl knew that rushing through the bedtime routine would only result in Ruth catching on to her urgency and not settling down and then likely waking little Abigail too.

Besides, she loved these moments with her girls. Even if she was exhausted from the week. She tucked Ruth's hair behind her ears and bent to give her a hug and kiss. "Okay, precious. Good night. I love you."

"Night night." Ruth snuggled into her blankets, so Pearl stood, switched off the lamp on the bedside table, and got two whole steps away before Ruth's next, "Mama?"

"Yes, baby?" She didn't stop moving toward the door though she paused once she reached it. Another part of the routine. Ruth was always full of questions at bedtime and would ask them indefinitely if Pearl let her.

"Will baby sleep in here?"

"I don't know yet. It depends on if it's a boy or a girl." They had one more bedroom in their little bungalow. It served as the guest room now, but it would become either Ruth's room or the baby's, depending. "If it's a girl, she and Abigail will sleep in here and you'll get your own room. Remember?"

"Like this room."

Two days ago she'd been excited at the thought of a room of her own. But then, she was a toddler. They weren't known for their steadfast opinions. "Okay. We'll see. Night night, sweetie."

"Night. Mama?"

Funny how her kids could make sighs and smiles battle for their place on her lips. "Good night, Ruth."

"One more question!"

"One more." Her little one's favorite phrase, it seemed.

"We make cookies tomorrow?"

Pearl chuckled. Cookie was the word Ruth chose for any sweet, and boy did she have a sweet tooth. She was always wanting cakes or cookies or candy. Maybe they'd been a bit too liberal with the baked goods after the sugar rationing finally lifted. Although to be fair, Pearl had quite a taste for sweets with this pregnancy, so she didn't exactly argue much when Ruth asked for more. "Sure, baby. Night night."

She slipped out the door before another "one more" could be asked, smiling as she walked down the short hallway and emerged into the living room.

Howard was already perched on the edge of the couch, fiddling with the radio. She'd had it on her favorite station for music during the day, but that wasn't the one they wanted now. As he turned the dial, voices and music slid into and back out of range in a strange tangle that finally clarified into a familiar prelude.

Pearl checked her watch. Eight o'clock on the dot. She had enough time to grab a glass of iced tea from the fridge without missing anything vital. Picking up her pace a bit, she heard the familiar tagline of their favorite mystery show come over the music. Pearl mouthed along with it. "In the windy city, mysteries abound, but none whose answer can't be found by this intrepid duo, lovely Josie and her big brother, Joe..."

She poured her tea and debated whether to take the time to grab a snack—then spotted the cracker box on the counter. Howard must have already gotten a plate ready for them to share. Excellent. She hurried back into the living room and eased down on the cushion beside him just as the last bars of the intro music faded out.

Howard lifted the plate of cheese and crackers and grapes from the end table and set it between them with a grin.

"Thanks." Even now, in her sixth month, she had trouble eating in the morning without feeling sick, so most of her food *was consumed in the second half of the day. A bedtime snack had become the order of business.*

Heavy footsteps sounded on the airwaves, and the squeaking of a door. Most episodes started this way, though not all of them—with a new client coming into the offices of J&J, Private Investigators. Pearl reached for a slice of cheese and a cracker.

The door slammed shut, and a gruff voice said, "Looking for Joe. Joe Johnson, Private I. This the right place?"

"So says the letters on the door." This voice was Josie's, bored and a little condescending.

"You his secretary?"

"Sure." Amusement, now, in her tone. She was always mistaken for the secretary, and she'd given up trying to convince their male clients that she was the other J—though when women came to them, they believed it easily enough. "But Joe's out right now. If you wanna—"

"Listen, gal, I ain't got time to wait for your boss to get back. I got people after me. Dangerous people. You get what I'm sayin'?"

A squeak, like a chair made when someone shifted their weight in it. "Sure, I hear ya. But this ain't the bullpen, champ. You're in that kinda trouble, you'd be better off going to the police."

"Can't. They're involved, or one of 'em is. Don't know who to trust. But Joe Johnson, he's got a reputation, see."

"Don't I know it." Josie's voice was dry now, but she was amused again. Joe always got the credit for solving the cases even when it was mostly her, and even when he tried to tell people that. They rarely listened.

"Well listen, Mr...?"

"Smith."

"Mr. Smith. Joe should be back in about twenty minutes, but if you're in a hurry, you can give me the details you need him to have and what you want him to do for you. Now don't look at me like that—this is my job. Taking down all the pertinent information on new cases. See?"

"Fine, fine." The scraping of a chair over the office floor and then the sound of a large figure sitting.

Pearl took a bite of her cracker and closed her eyes, calling to mind the image she'd created of the P.I. office based on the picture they'd painted with words and sounds. There were two rooms—this outer room that Josie called her own, and then the "inner sanctum" that was Joe's office. Hers had the main door and opened into a hallway that led to stairs. His had a window overlooking the alley with blinds that rattled whenever he looked outside. And somewhere or another was a little water closet, of course.

In her mind, the whole office was in shades of brown, though she wasn't sure why she saw it that way. Maybe because the floors sounded like wood, as did the desks? And even the desk chairs—they squeaked like the one Howard had at the little desk in their bedroom, and it was wooden, on casters.

There'd be some color somewhere though. Josie liked color. She was always being described as "the dame in the red dress" or blue or yellow or green. No browns and grays and blacks for her. So maybe she'd have brought in chairs with a splash of color or had an emerald-green ink blotter on her desk, at least.

This new fellow, though. Pearl imagined him in dark colors.

Paper rattled. "Okay, Mr. Smith. Let's start with why you have dangerous men chasing you, shall we?"

Howard leaned a little closer to the radio, like he always did when the first details of the case were spilled. For good reason—crucial details were always contained in these first few minutes, and all the main players would be introduced by the twenty-minute mark. He always tried to guess who the culprit was by the time the show went into its second commercial break.

Often, he was right. Pearl never tried to guess. It was more fun for her just to listen and see how the show progressed, what surprises came up, and what clues Josie and Joe picked up on that would lead them to the solution. Pearl was no private investigator, but she was getting better at noticing which details were important. She just didn't always know why they were important.

For instance, after this Mr. Smith explained that he'd accidentally gotten on the bad side of a certain mobster, there came a clatter of something falling to the ground, and Josie asked what he'd dropped. "Oh, this? Nothing," he said. "Just a pen. Nervous habit, twirling it, you know."

A pen. Innocuous, but nothing made it into the hour that wasn't important. That pen, or the fact that he had it with him, or that he twirled it, would come into play again. Every detail counted. She just didn't know how yet.

The crackers and cheese and grapes all vanished before the second commercial break, at which point Howard turned to her, his eyes gleaming. "The cabby. It was the cabby who set him up."

Pearl made a face. "You think? I like him though. Maybe it's that waitress."

"Nah. The waitress is just grumpy because her husband's a deadbeat and she doesn't appreciate being treated on the job like she's treated at home."

The only other characters they'd met so far were a grandmother and her eight-year-old grandson, and she couldn't imagine it was one of them who had set up Smith to take the fall with a gangster—though stranger things had happened on the show—so Pearl sighed out her defeat and leaned into Howard's side. "Fine, the cabby."

It was, of course, the cabby. Howard hooted his pleasure when the big reveal proved him right.

Pearl cast a glance down the hall, chuckling even as she shushed him. But there were no noises from the girls' room, so no harm done with his hoot. Most times they didn't stir during the Windy City hour, but once in a while they surprised her and she ended up missing a few minutes while she resettled them.

Although...that was odd. There were still five minutes left. Usually, they didn't wrap it up this early. Was there more to the ending than the cabby after all? She checked her watch and then showed it to Howard.

Howard frowned. "Five minutes early. Is there—but no, there's the music."

The final melody did indeed come on just then, though it faded out again quickly. "This is Heath Reynolds, the voice of Joe Johnson," the actor said in that smooth baritone that worked so well on air. "I'm here to tell all of our wonderful listeners about a little something new we're doing. In a departure from our normal one-hour mysteries, next week we'll be introducing a mystery that will span several episodes—five, to be exact—and which will culminate in a grand finale that we just know you're going to love."

"I'll say," said Josie—or rather, "This is Betty Gardiner, and let me chime in to say that this is a real exciting endeavor. Instead of filming the next few weeks in Chicago, like we usually do—"

"We're going to be on location, as it were. Josie and Joe will be traveling away from the Windy City after next week's episode, and we thought—"

"Why not record on location? In each city they go to?" Betty laughed, making Pearl wonder whose idea it had been. "Isn't that fun, folks?"

"By the end of next week's episode, clever sleuths will be able to deduce which city our duo is heading to next. Any fans who want to meet the cast and crew will be able to do so at the radio station in that city on the following Monday and then around town throughout the week."

"That's right, Heath, and we'll also be hosting a live listening party on Friday nights at eight o'clock before we move on to the next city. Details about locations will appear in the local newspaper."

"Just our way of thanking you, our listeners, for making this little show a big success. We wouldn't be here solving mysteries every week if it wasn't for you."

Pearl knew her mouth hung open, but she was shocked. Chicago wasn't that far away. If the cast and crew left the Windy City and perhaps headed southwest, that could put them within driving distance of Canton.

She turned wide eyes on Howard. "You hear that? We might be able to meet them! If they got close enough one week, maybe my parents would watch the girls and we could go for the listening party. Wouldn't that be fun?"

Howard nodded and then pointed at the radio. Betty was talking again.

"And we have one more surprise. The finale to this little five-part series has a few guest roles that haven't been cast yet. If you can solve the mystery before the fifth show airs and can get yourself to Kansas City the first week of March, you can audition for one of those roles!"

"Oh, now you just let a little bit of the secret slip, Betty." Heath's laugh, though, said that "slip" was planned. "That's right, folks, this mystery's ultimate solution will be found in Kansas City, and tickets to the live recording of that episode will be available for purchase from your local call stations or by phoning our producers here in Chicago. You'll be able to get your tickets to the show starting tomorrow."

A live recording! Plenty of comedy acts recorded before a live audience, and a lot of music shows did too. But this one had never been live before.

"We hope to see you there!" Heath and Betty said together.

The music struck up again, and Pearl and Howard turned to each other. Howard's eyes were bright, his expression both thoughtful and excited. "Think your parents would want to watch the kids for a couple days? Kansas City isn't that far. We could drive it. A trip with just the two of us before the baby comes?"

A thrill coursed through her, quickly followed by the cold dousing of reality. Kansas City wasn't that far when she could sit for more than an hour at a clip without needing to move around and change positions and when she didn't have to visit the ladies' room every two minutes. But at seven months pregnant, it didn't sound quite so fun. She rubbed a hand over her stomach, where a little hand or foot was pressing.

Howard's smile went soft and understanding. "We could play that one by ear. See how you're feeling in a month. Though it would be something to be on the show, wouldn't it?"

She hadn't even considered that part. "Not me," she said with a laugh. "Besides, I'm never the one to solve the mystery. You could though. I bet you'll have it all sorted out by episode two. And there's no reason you couldn't go audition, even if I don't feel up to coming along."

"Nah." Howard rested his hand over hers, over the moving bump of baby, and smiled. "I wouldn't leave you here alone with the kids for something like that. But maybe the show will come close to us, like you said. We could catch one of the Friday evening events. That would be swell."

"Wouldn't it? Let's just hope they're not going all over the country. If they're starting in Chicago and ending in Kansas City, it seems like our chances could be pretty good."

"Let's hope so." Howard dropped a kiss onto her head and tucked her into her usual place against his side, his arm slung over her shoulders. "Regardless, it'll be fun to see if we can figure out where they're going next."

Pearl chuckled her agreement and snuggled in while the radio switched to the next hour's programming. She had no doubt at all that Howard would have it mapped out the minute they dropped the clues.

Now she just had to figure out either how to talk him into auditioning for that role without her or how to make a five-hour car ride more comfortable.

Chapter Four

*T*racy juggled a tray of coffees in one hand and a box of pastries from Buttermilk Bakeshop in the other, pushing the door to the newspaper office open with her hip. When Annette caught sight of her, she jumped up from her desk to take the box of goodies—just in time, because Tracy's purse was slipping off the shoulder of her puffer coat and was about to make things difficult.

"Thanks, Annette." She slid the coffees onto the first handy surface and adjusted her purse.

Annette was already peeking under the cheerful pink cardboard lid. "Ooh, these look good. Are we celebrating something, or did you just want to sweeten up our Monday?"

"I was in the mood and know better than to arrive without enough to share. Hey, Bethany," she said when the reporter walked by, her nose buried in a printout. "Buttermilk delivery."

Always enough to inspire a detour. Jake, Edmund, and Eric all answered the call while Tracy stowed her stuff at her desk and shrugged out of her coat. She wished everyone good morning, claimed her own coffee and a donut, and then powered up her computer.

She already had this week's column mostly done. It was, in fact, part two of a series she'd begun last week about Canton's most spectacular weddings. She owed a tip of her hat to Amy for that idea, of course. The *Lewis County Times* had covered many a wedding in its history, and some of the write-ups were pretty fantastic. As were some of the photographs. She had enough material to keep the series going through Valentine's Day, which seemed appropriate.

The number of emails sitting in her inbox, and the encouraging subject lines, assured her that the topic was well received, at least by the female portion of the population. She had a few emails from guys too, which could go either way. She clicked on one with the subject line *In response to last week's column*, and held her breath while it loaded.

She let it out again with a relieved whoosh when she saw that the man had been a guest at the wedding she'd featured from the 1950s and that he recalled it being great fun.

Excellent. She'd been afraid she'd come in this morning and find that the initial positive responses of Thursday and Friday last week had given way to a mountain of complaints at the idea of the theme continuing for two more weeks. But that didn't seem to be the case. There was one email that simply said, *I was never much for weddings. Awful lot of money spent on a single day.* But that was the extent of the reader's opinion, so she decided not to let it deter her.

Relieved, Tracy sipped her coffee and ate her donut while she brought up the column she'd drafted for this Wednesday's edition, reading through what she had so far, tweaking and editing as she went. She perused the original article in the paper she'd fished out of the archives, checked a couple facts, and smiled at the truly mind-boggling wedding cake that was pictured in the write-up. She set it aside to scan. That photo had to go in her column. No question about it.

By lunchtime, she'd emailed the column to Annette for her editorial eyes and was just about to take the newspaper back down to the basement when Eric paused at her desk, rapping a knuckle on the corner to announce himself.

"Hey, had a thought."

She swiveled her chair to face him, brows lifted. "Glad to hear it."

He glared at her playfully for a second before his face relaxed again. "Last week's wedding-from-the-past feature was well-received."

He didn't phrase it as a question, which probably meant that plenty of reader mail had come in to the general *Times* email address and possibly even to his, not just to her own. She nodded. "Yep, everyone seems to be enjoying it. That's why I figured I'd keep it going until Valentine's Day."

"Keep it going all month, if you have enough material. Actually, my thought was that you should do a smaller version for the online edition. One a day would be perfect. And all the *more* perfect if you find couples who are still together and alive. It could be a celebration of Canton's senior couples, all through the month."

"Oh, that's good. That's I-wish-I'd-thought-of-it good." Tracy swiveled back around to jot the idea on a piece of paper. "I could get word out that we're looking for Canton's oldest couples, get their names and wedding dates, and then dive into the archives to search out the original wedding announcements and articles."

"Exactly." Eric drummed his fingers on her desk and finished the drumroll with a silent cymbal crash that pointed at her. "Knew you'd jump on it. I'll leave you to it. Let me know if you need anything. Otherwise, just run wherever it takes you."

"Will do." She could start with some of her own neighbors and couples from church. Ask them who they knew, start collecting names. She could probably scrape a quick something together to go onto the website tomorrow and tack a call for nominations for features on the end of it.

This was going to be fun. A little more time-consuming than she was hoping for this week—it would definitely eat into her radio-mystery-solving time—but job before play, she supposed. She once again picked up the newspaper she needed to return to the archives.

"But the digimitized ones don't go back far enough."

Tracy paused, her attention grabbed by the mispronunciation of *digitized*. A rather cute mispronunciation, which reminded her of how one of her nieces might say it—only that was definitely not a kid's voice. She headed toward Annette's office and spotted a head full of white curls on a little body standing in the doorway.

Annette nodded. "I do realize our digitized archives only go back to the seventies, ma'am. But we simply can't allow the public into our physical archives."

That was the truth. Those steep steps that led to the basement were reason number one they didn't let just anyone look through their collection. And the lack of preservation was the second. Most of the "archives" were haphazard piles of old papers, and while they all tried to bring a little order to the place when they had cause to go down there, it was still quite a mess. Some issues were encased in plastic sleeves but most were not. Which meant every time someone touched one, a little more damage was done.

Hence, no public in the archives.

But Tracy would be spending lots of time in the basement this month, from the sounds of it. She approached Annette and their visitor with a smile. "Hi. Can I maybe help with something?"

The white-haired, brown-skinned woman turned to look at her and offered a big smile. "You're that columnist—I recognize your photo. The Canterbury Tales lady."

"Cantonbury." She didn't *mean* to correct the woman. It just slipped out. She covered it with a smile. "Yep, that's me. Is there something you're looking for in our archives, ma'am? I might be able to search for it for you while I'm down there." She held up the paper from 1955 as proof of her access.

"Oh, aren't you a dear for offering?" Though instead of smiling, the woman narrowed her eyes at her. "I'll need you to sign one of those what's-its—a non-disclosing thingy."

Tracy had to blink for a few moments. "A nondisclosure? Um…I don't think I can promise not to disclose something that's in the newspaper archives. It's already public knowledge." She cast a glance at Annette, though she wasn't sure if she was asking for help or maybe just more information.

Annette seemed to be holding back a grin. She shrugged.

"Well, but that's the thing, isn't it? It's *not* public knowledge. Because it's not digimitized."

"But whichever articles you're looking for are probably on microfiche at the library. They have a pretty complete—"

"Oh, who wants to read anything in those funny machines?" The woman waved that off. "No one I know. And I can guarantee you it's the people I know that'll be coming here any minute, trying to get at these articles. I need you to promise me that you'll give me the—what do you news people call it? The inside scoop? Exclusive rights?"

Oh, boy. Tracy renewed her smile and hoped it was placating. "Sorry, ma'am, but I really can't promise something like that. Why don't you come back to my desk, and you can tell me what information you're looking for? I think the first step is just figuring out if we have it."

The woman followed Tracy to her desk. When Tracy glanced back, she caught the woman looking over her shoulder as if she expected a whole busload of people to come barging into the building at any moment, demanding archival access.

Tracy pulled out a chair for her. "Let's start with your name."

"Mrs. Darla Franklin." Mrs. Franklin sat, though she scooted the chair around to keep an eye on the door. "And I just *know* that Mary Jane Shoemaker is going to be here any second."

"Well, if she shows up, you can bet Annette won't let her into the archives either, and I doubt anyone else is going to volunteer to do a search—unless it's an emergency? Something really important?"

Mrs. Franklin relaxed a bit. "Not an emergency, no. Though I certainly think it's important." She turned to face Tracy. "I have to win that river cruise. It would be just perfect for our anniversary."

Tracy dragged in a long breath. "Ah. The *Turn Back the Dial* contest, I take it?"

Mrs. Franklin's eyes lit—and then went shrewd. "You know about it? I didn't think anyone as young as you even listened to that show."

"We turn it on every now and then. My husband suggested we listen this last weekend."

"Do you mean to enter? To solve the mystery?"

Why did answering feel so cruel? But she couldn't lie. She nodded.

"Oh." The woman visibly deflated. "Well then. *You* have access to the archives, so I guess that's that on that lead."

"Hold on a second," Tracy said when Mrs. Franklin stood, shoulders a good deal more stooped than they'd been a moment ago. "The way I see it, what was in the news in 1949 ought to be public knowledge—and would be, if we had our archives digitized and online. So how about this. I'll be the emissary who goes down there and searches, but I'll share what I find with any other contest hopefuls."

Mrs. Franklin frowned at her. "Why would you do that?"

Why indeed? Tracy shrugged. "It doesn't seem fair that I'd have access to information no one else does just because I work here. And besides, according to Ken, the mystery was unsolved in 1949. That would mean that nothing in those articles is going to give us the actual solution. It'll only bring us all up to date on the mystery."

"Even Mary Jane Shoemaker." Mrs. Franklin sighed. "Well, that's more than fair, dear. But maybe… Could you give it only to those who come asking? I mean…you're not going to put it up on the inter-webs, are you? For anyone to see? I had my Stewie searching for me yesterday. That's how I know the old papers aren't digimitized."

Tracy nodded. "That seems perfectly fair. We'll share the information with anyone who asks, but only with those who ask."

"Deal." Mrs. Franklin held out a hand, eyes alight again.

Tracy shook her hand. "Deal. Now." She reached for her note-book and pen. "It's going to take me some time to find anything useful down there. To be quite honest, the archives aren't as orga-nized as we'd like them to be. Let me know the best way to reach you, and I'll let you know when I've found anything useful." Recall-ing those shrewd eyes, she added, "If you don't hear from me this afternoon, feel free to call or swing by again tomorrow. I promise I won't just take the information and run away, but I *do* have columns to work on, so I can't guarantee this will get done by any set time."

"Understood, understood." Though rather than reach for the pen and paper, she instead opened her purse, fished around for a moment, and came out with a business card. "Here you go."

Tracy took the card, her brows lifting at the gold-foil design. *Darling Darla Designs ~ Custom Dresses for All Occasions.* "You're a seamstress?"

Mrs. Franklin flexed her hand. "Not as much these days as I used to be, thanks to arthritis and general slowing-down. But I am indeed. I opened my doors in 1964. First paying job I had at Darling Darla's was a wedding gown—prettiest, craziest thing I ever made. And you can tell that Mary Jane Shoemaker I said so too."

"Uh." She didn't know if that meant the dress had been Mary Jane's, or if Mary Jane had strong opinions on some *other* creation that deserved the title. Either way, she wrote down the year and the name. "You know, we're going to be featuring weddings and married couples in the paper all through February. I don't suppose you have any tips on who we should feature?"

"Oh, you bet I do!" But instead of leaning forward, she stood, looking like the cat that ate the canary. "I'll just make a list for you, all right? And then we can trade. Information, I mean. I'll give you the inside scoop on last century's weddings, and you can let me know what you find out about that radio show fella."

Maybe it would have rankled to be distrusted if the woman didn't say it with such a sweet attitude. And if, frankly, it wasn't a perfectly fair trade. "You have a deal on that too. I'll just give you a call here when I have something." She waved the card.

"There's an email address on there too. My daughter checks it. She's the main seamstress at the shop these days and runs all the computer stuff. Only thing I'll do on one of those contraptions is play my card game. Don't need it for anything else."

Tracy chuckled. "Solitaire?"

"FreeCell."

"All right. Well, one way or another, you'll hear from me soon." She held out a hand to shake. "I look forward to our little partnership here, Mrs. Franklin."

"Oh, call me Darla, sweetie. Everyone does." She gripped Tracy's hand firmly.

"And I'm Tracy."

"I'll talk to you soon, Tracy."

Tracy stood there for a moment after Darla had left, tapping the card against her palm. Darla Franklin was, unless her instincts were failing her, what Grandma Pearl had always called a firecracker. Tracy liked her already.

She stored the business card in a drawer, picked up the paper again, and actually made it to the basement this time without getting sidetracked. First she put away the paper she'd had out, and then she took a wild guess as to which stack might contain editions from February of 1949.

She guessed wrong. Sighing, she nevertheless paged through the Society sections of the stack she'd pulled down, on the lookout for any extravagant or interesting weddings in 1962. After setting a couple issues aside, she went back to her search.

It took twenty minutes just to find the stack that contained the papers from February and March of 1949, but at least once she had them out, she didn't need to rustle through every page to know which ones she needed. For a whole week, the radio stars dominated the front page, first because of their arrival in town and then because of Heath's disappearance. Curiously, though, it all went from front-page news to...nothing. No more mentions in the weeks to follow, on the front page or anywhere else. She added the helpful issues to her pile to be carried upstairs then spent a little more time looking for weddings.

When she finally reemerged from the basement after two trips up and down the stairs, the office was quiet. The others, it seemed, had all left for lunch. Even thinking about that made her stomach growl, so she heated up the soup she'd brought and ate it while she read a few more online articles about Betty Gardiner and Heath Reynolds.

The conclusion she was coming to, the more she looked, was that somehow Heath Reynolds had managed to avoid all publicity that would someday make it onto the internet. She wasn't sure how anyone in broadcasting had pulled that off, but the results were undeniable. He scarcely appeared anywhere, and most of the information was about how he vanished, though no foul play was ever in evidence.

Once she finished her lunch, she got back down to business. First up, of course, would have to be finding some couples and weddings to highlight on the website this week. But before she left for the day, she intended to scan the papers she'd found from 1949 so she could review the information at home on her own time...and get it to any other contestants who came knocking.

Chapter Five

Annette's voice reached Tracy as she shut down her computer for the day, raised in a way Tracy had seldom heard. At first the words themselves weren't all that clear, but as she stepped closer, they clarified.

"As I already told you, ma'am, we don't let the public into the archives. Now, if you'll sit down, I believe one of our employees may already be researching this—"

"For who?" The second voice was feminine, sharp. "Who was in here already? Nancy Kramer? Or was it Darla Franklin? Oh, I bet it was the Clarks, wasn't it?"

"I don't know, ma'am."

Tracy stepped into sight, her coat already on and purse over her shoulder. She'd gotten half of the papers from 1949 scanned in, but unless she wanted to stay here all evening—which she didn't—the rest would have to wait until tomorrow.

Seeing the way Annette physically blocked the older woman from charging down the hallway, Tracy was suddenly glad she'd put the papers in her desk drawer. Just a precaution to keep them from blowing around in any stray drafts or being put away by a helpful colleague before she was ready. But the tall woman wearing a teal coat and matching scarf who tried to push past Annette looked like she wouldn't be above snatching the papers from Tracy's desk and running away with them.

"Annette? Anything I can help with?" Tracy hurried to her friend, ready to provide backup if necessary. The woman appeared to be around seventy, and if the look on her face was anything to go by, she was used to getting her own way.

The visitor glared at her. "You can't keep me from it, you know. It's *news*. Public record. I demand to see the 1949 archives, this instance." She tried again to barge past Annette, who moved with her, blocking the way, arms outstretched.

Tracy wondered where all the men had gotten to. Not that she could imagine any of them tackling a seventy-year-old woman, but... She filled the gap Annette left on the other side. "Actually, ma'am, yes, you're right, the news itself is public record, but our archives are private property, owned by Doug Ledger and the *Lewis County Times*. Our policy is that no one but staff goes into the archives. I've already pulled some of the 1949 papers out of storage, and I'll be scanning them over the next few days and making copies available to anyone who asks."

In her head she could hear Darla Franklin saying, *"Even Mary Jane Shoemaker."* She narrowed her eyes. "Are you by chance—?"

"Mary Jane Shoemaker." The woman lifted her chin in a way that made Tracy wonder what her profession had been in her younger years. She'd have believed the woman had been a quarterback or a lawyer based on her demeanor.

"Ah." Darla could have warned her a little more explicitly. She forced herself to smile. "If you'll leave your contact information, I'll let you know as soon as all the scans have been completed and the copies are ready. The same information will be made available to everyone."

The woman sniffed. "You expect me to believe that?"

Annette must have deemed it safe to relax her stance a bit. She folded her arms over her chest and gave Mrs. Shoemaker a glare of her own. "Mrs. Shoemaker, you're welcome to check the library's microfiche collection and pay for copies. Or you can wait patiently, just like all the other contestants."

"All?" Mrs. Shoemaker came to attention again. "Who else was here already?"

Tracy made a "calm down" gesture with her hands, even though she didn't think it would do any good. "I don't feel comfortable revealing that information, nor will I tell others that *you* were here."

Mrs. Shoemaker gave her a once-over and didn't seem to like what she saw. "Fine. I'll give you my phone number and email address. And you can be sure I'll be checking what you provide against the library's microfiche collection."

Tracy very nearly advised the woman to save them all the trouble and just head to the library, but that didn't feel very gracious. So she made herself refresh her smile and led her over to the pen and paper waiting on a desk.

There were a couple of other names listed there already in Annette's handwriting—the very ones Mrs. Shoemaker had spat out. Tracy flipped the page so the woman wouldn't see them and took down her contact info.

"You can expect to hear from me tomorrow or Wednesday," she then said, working to keep her tone pleasant. "I can't make promises on when, exactly, since I have work that needs to be done first for the *Times*."

The woman's snort sounded more like doubt than anything. "I just bet."

Good grief, why was she being so nasty? Tracy clamped her teeth together to keep from saying anything more and held her expression in as neutral a mask as she could manage until the door closed behind the woman. Then she let out a gust of breath.

"That one's a piece of work." Annette shook her head and stepped into her office long enough to grab her coat and purse. "The others who came in this afternoon while you hid in the archives were all sweetness and light. I didn't at all mind taking down their information. But *that* one. Yikes."

"You've got that right."

"Why is everyone so excited about this thing anyway? The contest? What's it about?"

Tracy sighed. "A river cruise is the prize."

Annette let out a whistle, her eyes going wide. "I researched those last year. They can cost thousands of dollars."

"I know." It certainly wasn't a weekend at a B and B or tickets to a play or something. Though it made her wonder how the radio show had scored such a prize. Had the cruise company donated two tickets?

She'd see if Jeff knew. Maybe Ken had told him. She wasn't sure *why* the cruise line would be so eager to sponsor a contest like this, but maybe they had a themed event coming up they wanted attention for or maybe they needed the tax write-off. The college radio station was nonprofit.

Although Ken hadn't said the contest was sponsored by anyone in particular. Usually when something was, promotion was part of the gig.

"I'm kinda surprised we haven't heard from WFWM, asking us to include the contest in this week's paper." Annette set her purse down so she could slide her arms into her coat sleeves.

"Yeah, that is a little odd. Don't we normally list their activities in the community calendar?"

"Mm-hmm." Annette arranged her collar and picked her purse up again. "Maybe they just missed the advertising and calendar deadlines for this week's edition. I'll try to remember to send Ken a quick note tomorrow, to see if he wants it included in next week's."

Next week's edition would come out on Valentine's Day, and readers who hadn't heard Saturday's program would only have three days before the winner was announced. Didn't seem like it would be worth it to advertise the contest that late. Though who was she to say? "I'll remind you if you forget."

"Appreciate it. Any plans tonight?"

"Just dinner and listening to the next episode for the contest. Robin and Terry are coming over again to listen with us."

She and Annette walked out together, chatting about the weekend and dinner plans, and parted ways at their cars.

A few minutes later, she pulled into a parking spot at the library and gathered the three novels she needed to return. She deposited them on the counter as she walked in, smiling at Grace Park, the head librarian, then headed for a computer that had the catalog up.

Though not entirely certain what she hoped to find, she did a few searches for old radio shows and the names of the two stars. There wasn't exactly a wealth of titles available at the Canton library, but she jotted down the Dewey Decimal numbers for what they had and moved toward the nonfiction section.

A flash of teal caught her eye. She turned, but she didn't see anything other than rows of shelves and a few not-teal-clad patrons.

She blinked and shook her head. Must have been her imagination. She was probably paranoid after that encounter with Mary Jane Shoemaker.

On with her task. She found the three titles she was looking for, a bit surprised none of the women who had come to the paper today had beat her to them. She stacked them up and browsed nearby sections just to make sure nothing else caught her eye. She added a twentieth-century fashion book to her stack. If she was going to describe wedding gowns this month, she could stand to brush up on some of the verbiage.

That should do. Four books in hand, she'd made it halfway to the counter when her phone buzzed in her purse.

When the ringtone for Jeff sang out a second later, she winced. Not at Jeff calling, of course, but, even muffled by her coat, it sounded loud in the quiet of the library. She hadn't thought to silence it when she came in. She slid the books onto a table and pulled out the phone, declining the call to get the ringing to stop. She tapped the message icon and typed out, SORRY, IN THE LIBRARY. WHAT'S UP? While she typed, she turned toward the shelves to block the glare of the fluorescent lights on her screen.

The little bubbles danced to let her know he was typing a reply, though it seemed to take a long time before it finally popped up on her screen. TALKED TO KEN FOR A WHILE TODAY. TOO MUCH TO TYPE. I'LL BE HOME AROUND 5.

That sounded intriguing. She typed SEE YOU SOON and then slid her phone back into her purse. She turned to pick up her books again...and frowned.

There was nothing on the table but the slips of paper and the basket of pencils that were always there. No books. Where were her books?

Teal caught her eye again, and she looked up to see Mary Jane Shoemaker at the checkout desk, smiling at the librarian and drumming her fingers on the counter, clearly impatient. She glanced at Tracy then quickly averted her eyes.

Tracy's jaw dropped when she saw the books the woman was checking out—*her* books!

Okay, not hers, they were the public library's, but still. She had just pulled them off the shelf minutes ago. Tracy marched toward the counter, not exactly sure what she meant to say but already preparing her whisper-shout to say it in.

Mrs. Shoemaker tossed a smug little smile at her and in three steps was through the front door. Tracy buttoned her lips against the words of frustration she wanted to spew. The thieving woman could have at least left her the fashion book—*that* wouldn't serve any purpose for her.

Even though she was empty-handed now, she still followed her preset course and ended up at the counter.

Grace gave her a curious look. "Hey, Tracy. Need help finding something?"

"No." She couldn't restrain the huff of breath. "I found what I needed, but that woman—Mary Jane Shoemaker?—swiped them from the table when I wasn't looking and checked them out herself."

Grace's eyes went wide. "Wow, okay. That doesn't happen often. I mean, not outside of the toddlers in Story Time now and again."

That analogy made Tracy chuckle, which in turn brought the situation into perspective. She shrugged. "Oh well. If she wants them that badly... But consider yourself warned. You may have some overeager people asking about the microfiche in the next week or so."

Grace frowned. "Mrs. Shoemaker asked about that too. Like I told her, we don't have any of that anymore."

That gave Tracy pause. "What? Didn't you used to?"

"Sure, but no one was using them. We phased them out and now just have the digital archives instead, accessible online to anyone with a library card. Gives you access to more than forty newspapers and all their back editions."

But that meant nothing earlier than the '70s for the *Times*, since that was as far as they'd gotten in the quest to convert their archives to digital. Tracy sighed. "Well, so much for sending people here. Sorry about that."

Grace shrugged. "No problem. Sorry about the swiped books."

Tracy mirrored her shrug. "You couldn't have known. I'd better get home. See you later, Grace."

"Have a great week."

Zipping her jacket up to her chin, Tracy walked back to her car, wondering if she should check the tires for slashes. She rolled her eyes at her own paranoia. Mary Jane Shoemaker might not be above nabbing someone else's library books, but surely she wasn't that vindictive—especially having "won" that last battle, if that was what it was.

She kept replaying the day over in her mind as she drove home. When she called or emailed Darla Franklin, she'd have to see what she could learn about Mrs. Shoemaker, just so she'd know what to expect. Somehow, she wouldn't be surprised if she saw a teal coat everywhere she turned over the next few days.

Clearly the woman didn't trust her and viewed her as competition—which she *was*, of course. But wasn't this a friendly contest? Even with a prize worth thousands of dollars, there was no call for being rude.

Chapter Six

Though tempted to simmer over the incident in the library, Tracy drew in a deep breath when she pulled into the driveway. She said a prayer for renewed peace as she parked and took Sadie out then turned some upbeat praise music on while she got out the ingredients for dinner and started cooking. Nothing got her out of a funk like singing about how good God was.

By the time Jeff came in, the kitchen was fragrant with the scent of onions and garlic and she was smiling again.

He came over for a kiss and peeked into the pot. "That smells good."

"Chicken tetrazzini, I was thinking."

"No arguments here. Hey, I had a crazy question come to mind while I was talking to Ken. Think Grandma Pearl has any of her old radios up in the attic? He was saying how different the music and shows sound on vintage radios because they have vacuum tubes instead of solid-state components."

Tracy smiled and shrugged. "I have no idea if she kept any. But we can check after supper."

After he'd put his things away, Jeff returned to the kitchen to help finish up the cooking, and Robin and Terry soon arrived. Tracy welcomed them with a smile and entertained them with the stories of meeting Darla Franklin and Mary Jane Shoemaker, the telling of which proved far more humorous than the experience had been, in Mrs. Shoemaker's case.

Since it was just the four of them, they opted for the kitchen table instead of carrying everything into the dining room. Soon they were sitting down, blessing the food, and taking their first bites.

After a taste of the sauteed vegetables, Tracy asked Jeff, "So what was it you and Ken talked about that was too long to text? Just about old-fashioned radios?"

"Mostly that. Though he also mentioned that the contest was privately sponsored. He couldn't give details. He said it was all very mysterious and even he doesn't know who the sponsor is. All he knows is that last Friday afternoon, records of the show arrived along with two tickets to the river cruise and the parameters of the contest, to be announced that weekend."

"Whoa." Robin had just spooled a bite of noodles onto her fork but let it rest against her plate rather than raise it to her lips. "So out of the blue?"

Tracy frowned. "No wonder he didn't ask the paper to run anything about it."

"Didn't have a chance," he agreed with a chuckle, shaking his head. "Crazy, isn't it? He didn't believe it at first, he said. He spent Saturday on the phone verifying with the river cruise company that the tickets were genuine and doing some fact-checking about the show itself. He'd apparently never heard of it. And, as you well know, that's saying something."

Tracy took her next bite, brows knit. Ken was no older than Jeff, but he had a longstanding love of all things radio from the '30s and

'40s. He'd been emceeing the *Jukebox Saturday Night* show for twenty years, had added *Turn Back the Dial* to the lineup about five years ago, and apparently had a record collection that could be a museum exhibit. Throughout both shows, he peppered in factoids and history that made it clear this was a passion he pursued off the air too.

If he hadn't even known that *Windy City Gumshoes* existed, that was, as Jeff said, saying something. She just wasn't sure, exactly, *what* it was saying. "Has he learned more about it than he's already shared on the air?"

Jeff shrugged. "He's being careful with what he says. He doesn't want to give anyone an advantage in the contest. But he said he was more than a little surprised to see the 'Number 1 Mystery Show of 1948' badge on the record and then to find so little information about it online. He reads a lot of old articles about the music and entertainment of the day, you know, and had never come across it before."

"Weird."

Jeff nodded and polished off the last of his food, glancing at his watch. "Let's leave the dishes and head up to the attic. If there *is* a radio, I'd like to get it set up before tonight's broadcast."

"Sure. I'll just run the plates under some water and get the leftovers put away while you're fiddling, if there's anything to fiddle with."

Robin shook her head and reached for the plates. "Terry and I will clean up. You two go up to the attic. No need for us all to cram in there."

"You sure?" Tracy asked, hating to leave guests with the cleaning even if they weren't exactly *guests*.

Her cousin waved her on with a laugh. "Go."

"All right, all right." Tracy trailed Jeff to the attic stairs.

Cool air greeted them as they climbed, making her wish she'd thought to grab a sweater. The overhead bulbs cast their stark light on the boxes and tables and collections of memories. Tracy looked around once she was standing on the wooden planks of the attic floor, trying to remember if she'd seen a radio at any point. None stood out in her memory, but that didn't mean much. There were just so many things crammed into this space.

Jeff came up behind her, and he headed straight to the southeast corner. "I think I saw an old console radio back here once upon a time."

"Really?" She trailed him to the corner he'd selected, searching the shadows for anything promising. "I'll take your word for it."

Jeff crouched down, slid a few boxes out, and moved a few more things aside. "Here are some boxes marked 'favorite albums.' That sounds promising."

Tracy knelt in front of the two boxes he pushed toward her, angling her body to allow the light to hit them. The first one had a variety of records from the 1940s and '50s, their cardboard sleeves boasting every color of the rainbow and then some. She recognized many of the big names—Nat King Cole, Benny Goodman, Glenn Miller, Billie Holiday, Bing Crosby, and so on. Others were less familiar.

It all seemed to be music, so she pushed that one aside and tugged another box forward. "Oh, we may have something here." The first record she pulled out was *Fibber McGee and Molly*—a radio show, not music. "And a few magazine articles with interviews with the voice actors behind it, and even a poster."

The next few items were from a show called *Broadway Is My Beat*. She'd never heard of it, but it looked like a crime drama. After that was a rather large collection of *Blondie* memorabilia. "Huh." She pulled out the stack, bound together with a faded blue ribbon, of records, comic strips, articles, and who knew what else. "How did I not realize that Blondie and Dagwood Bumstead were on the radio back in the day?" The front of the record had a black-and-white picture of the two titular actors, clearly dressed for their roles. She flipped it over and saw that they were played by Arthur Lake and Penny Singleton. A few of the articles were about various feature films in the series.

She hadn't realized there were movies about the Bumsteads either, actually. In her mind they were simply comic-strip characters whose antics entertained generations. She remembered fighting with Amy when they were kids over who got to read the comics first on Sundays. *Blondie* was one of their favorites.

"Ha, knew it!" Jeff maneuvered something, the sound of wood-on-wood scraping filling the space. "Think it still works?"

She smiled at the classic-looking radio he pulled out. With its arched shape and scrollwork, it could have come straight from an old movie. "I have no idea if it does now, but you can bet it would have when Grandpa Howard put it up here."

Jeff winced a little as he examined the power cord. "Gotta love these old plugs. We'll just make sure there's a fire extinguisher handy."

Tracy chuckled. "They clearly didn't burn the house down with it before—though they were living in their first house in 1949, not this one."

"You know your grandparents. They would have kept using it even after they got a television and wouldn't have replaced it until they had to."

"True enough." She turned back to her box of favorite radio shows and gasped. "No way!"

"What?" Jeff hefted the radio.

"*Windy City Gumshoes!* They have…wow, quite a collection of records. Maybe all of them? I have no idea how many episodes are on each one. And there's articles, posters, even…" She trailed off, frowning as she pulled out a stack of white paper held together in the corner by a metal brad.

Jeff looked over his shoulder at her. "What?"

"I don't know. A script, maybe? The cover sheet says '*Windy City Gumshoes* Episode 152, The Case of the Other Joe.'"

"Want to bring it all down with you? We don't have a whole lot of time to get this working, if it even will."

"Sure." She put the *Blondie* things back in the box and gathered all of the *Windy City* stuff. On a whim, she detoured to an old record player whose location she knew and made it the base of her stack.

Jeff paused at the bottom of the stairs and waited for her to catch up. "Where do you think we should put this?"

"Ultimately the living room, but you might want to take it to the kitchen first so you can wipe it down. I'm sure it's pretty dusty."

"Good call."

Tracy followed him to the kitchen, knowing the same could be said for the vintage record player. For that matter, the stack of records had a fair coating of dust on their edges too.

Robin and Terry had all the food put away and the dishes done, so there was plenty of room on the table for the radio. Terry joined Jeff in bending over the old machine while Robin made a beeline for the box of memorabilia, eyes glinting. Tracy passed Jeff a damp paper towel and then moved to Robin's side.

"Grandma and Grandpa to the rescue again, huh?" Tracy glanced at the cover of the *Windy City* record that Robin pulled out.

Her cousin traced a finger along the sleeve's edge. "It's like that attic has the whole twentieth century stored away up there."

Jeff tossed the blackened paper towel into the trash can. "There. Clean...er."

Terry nodded. "And my cursory inspection of the innards didn't reveal anything frayed or an obvious fire hazard. Should we plug 'er in?"

"Go for it." Tracy did a mental check of where the fire extinguisher was in the room—just in case. From the discolored, ancient-looking plastic electric cord in Terry's hand, she could understand the guys' winces.

No sparks or crackles or anything else menacing greeted them when he plugged it in, so that boded well. Better still, when Jeff twisted one of the dials—it must have been the on/off switch because it just made a single click and moved ninety degrees—static filled the air. Static that morphed into country music when he turned another dial. "Hey!" Jeff hive-fived Terry.

"Nice!" Tracy moved to stand behind his chair. "I admit it. I'm surprised."

Jeff chuckled. "You and me both. I thought for sure I'd have to take it apart and tighten this and align that and try to figure out what everything did." He kept on turning the dial, taking them through the bands and several different stations before landing on 91.9. "With seven minutes to spare."

"More than enough time to set it up in the other room," Robin said. "Want me to help you clear a space for it, Tracy?"

"Sure." She and Sadie and Robin walked from the kitchen into the living room. Tracy went straight to the antique side table positioned under a window. She knew there was an outlet under it. "There, I think. We can move those framed photos, and the lamp can stay put."

Robin gathered up a few of the pictures, smiling. "You're going to have to order a frame that matches these so you can add Amy and Miles's wedding photo to the collection."

Tracy nodded. "I will."

"Where do you want these?"

She wasn't sure where she wanted to put them if she meant to banish them from this table for any length of time, but for now she directed Robin to scatter them throughout the room.

"By the lamp?" Jeff asked as he came in with the radio, Terry behind him.

"Yep, that should do."

"Great. If one of you wants to plug it in here and turn it back on and get your phone app ready to record, I'll get the boom box ready to record in the other room. We don't exactly need dueling radios on in here."

Tracy rolled her eyes at him. "Don't want a side-by-side sound comparison?"

"Not when we need to pay attention to what's being said rather than how it sounds." He left the plug sitting on the tabletop and spun for the eyesore of a black plastic boombox that they'd left on the floor by the couch after yesterday's show. "Be right back."

"Bring the stack of memorabilia in with you when you come!" With a bit of luck, Grandma Pearl and Grandpa Howard had these very episodes they were recording. Then they wouldn't have to worry about watching the clock every night. They could simply listen at their leisure. They could even finish them up tonight.

"Ooh, I'll grab that." Robin followed Jeff into the kitchen, returning a moment later with the box of records and magazines, which she deposited on the floor by the couch.

Terry plugged the vintage radio in, and Tracy pulled up the app on her phone and set it to record.

Jeff returned just as Ken finished up his introduction to the show. He cast an appreciative glance at the radio. "It *does* have a different sound quality, doesn't it?"

Did it? Maybe a little, though Tracy would have been hard-pressed to tell the difference in a blind study. She made an agreeable noise though and sat on the couch beside him while Robin and Terry claimed their usual chairs. Tracy reached for her notes from the previous two shows. Last night's had been the one with the clues that led the investigators—and the listeners—south from Chicago to Indianapolis. Tonight's was the first one recorded away from Chicago and, according to Ken's initial introduction, this one would drop clues leading them to Peoria. The one recorded there would air tomorrow night and send them *here*, to Canton.

Tracy was looking forward to that one and especially to the one after—the one recorded right here in town.

The mystery itself was riveting, she had to admit. They were searching for a missing heiress to "the coffee king," so while it was set entirely in the Midwest, there were fascinating tidbits included about the history of the coffee trade and the heiress's recent trip to Colombia. A hint of romance was even unfolding through the PIs' search. The missing young woman, Clair, was the daughter of the coffee importer, but on her trip to South America, she'd fallen in love with the owner of the plantation that was their primary supplier. Had she simply eloped with him? Or had a rival company kidnapped her? Or something else they hadn't yet considered?

Joe and Josie followed a trail that might have been Clair's last journey, but they couldn't be certain. She traveled frequently, all over the country, to her family's company's distribution centers. Most of the people the investigators interviewed reported that Clair was well loved, her visits highly anticipated affairs. She'd been dubbed "the coffee princess" and was especially beloved by veterans, who had drunk her family's joe all through the war. Many of them had stories of it warming them on cold nights in the trenches and how, when they'd come home, Clair and her father had held massive galas for them. The result was that their coffee brand had become *the* coffee brand for most of America.

They painted a convincing enough story that Tracy found herself wondering if Grandma Pearl and Grandpa Howard had used that brand of coffee—before remembering that it was entirely fictional.

"These are pretty good. I can see why it was so popular," Robin said after the episode was over.

"Agreed." Jeff got up to switch off the old radio then bent to pick up the rest of the albums. "But I'm beginning to think that Ken's 'that's for me to know and you to find out' tease about there being clues for the contest in these old episodes is a red herring."

"I'm leaning that way too," Tracy said. "It's a good way to distract contestants and at the same time boost ratings for the show. We're listening every night, just in case."

Jeff sat back down beside Tracy with the records in hand and began flipping through them. "Let's see... It looks like each record can only hold one episode. They must have just gotten their favorites. 'The Case of the Backward Bull,' 'The Case of the Pharaoh's Curse,' 'The Case of the Mobster's Dame.'"

"Well, phooey," Robin said. "I was hoping they'd all be there—guess that would have been a *lot* of records though. Clearly, I've been spoiled by CDs and DVDs with multiple episodes on each one." She went to the box of memorabilia and began looking through it.

"Yep." Jeff continued flipping through them, reading off more names as he went. None of them were ones Tracy recognized—not until the very last one in the stack, which Jeff read with raised brows. "Here we go—'The Case of the Coffee Princess, Part 4.' The one recorded here in Canton."

"Excellent. We could at least listen to that one early if we wanted." Rather than race for the record player though, Tracy took the magazine that Robin handed her.

November, 1948. She paged through it until she came to a section marked with a slip of paper. An article about the show, featuring a photo and an interview with Betty Gardiner. Tracy recognized her instantly.

This was clearly a professional glamor shot, Betty polished and posed. Tracy read the article with interest, learning far more in the two print pages than she had in all the online articles combined.

"Anything good?" Jeff asked a few minutes later.

"Yes, actually. Betty Gardiner had dreams of ending up on the silver screen before being cast for Josie. The radio gig was largely a stroke of luck. She'd auditioned for a part in a variety show in Chicago. She didn't get that gig, but when she was there, she met Heath Reynolds, who was one of the show's writers. He was about to pitch the concept for *Windy City Gumshoes* to the studio and asked if she'd like to be considered for the female lead. She says that they all thought it was a long shot, and that the mystery wouldn't be picked up."

"But it was," Terry said. He had his phone in his hand and was no doubt doing some online research.

"So it seems. She says, 'Thank heavens for Alfie Paulsen! His gamble sure paid off for us all, and I couldn't be more grateful.'"

"Alfie Paulsen?" Jeff wrote the name down on his notepad. "Must have been the producer or something."

"Maybe. This is interesting. When the interviewer asks her to talk more about Heath, she laughed and said, 'Oh, there's no man as private as Heath Reynolds! I don't dare tell you anything beyond what we all know—he's a stand-up guy, a great actor, and an even better writer. It's been great to work alongside him these last two years.'"

"Writer." Robin looked up from her stack of memorabilia, brows drawn. "So was he the writer of this show? Was it his idea?"

Tracy scanned the rest of the page to see if there was any summation of facts. "This article sure makes it sound that way, but I haven't seen anything about it anywhere else. The online articles didn't mention who the writer was. Which is kind of odd, now that I think about it."

"Not terribly uncommon for the star to have been the one to come up with it though, is it?" Robin asked. "I'm pretty sure that was the case for *Fibber McGee and Molly*'s lead actors, Jim and Marian Jordan."

Tracy returned to the place where she'd been reading. It was an interesting article but didn't really give her any other useful tidbits.

"Looks like your grandparents saved some newspapers too." Jeff pulled a couple pages of folded newsprint from the stack. She recognized the first of them immediately as one she'd already fetched from the archives, with the headline RADIO STARS IN CANTON.

Tracy leaned close to read it along with Jeff.

> *Many citizens of Canton thronged the studios of WFWM on Monday morning to welcome the arrival of the cast of the popular mystery program* Windy City Gumshoes, *which usually airs from their home studio of SongBird Records, the recording arm of WRMC in Chicago, Illinois.*
>
> *In a first for* Windy City, *as the characters chase clues around the Midwest, the show follows their path, recording each week's episode in the town in which the story is set. Fans of the mystery program were excited to realize during last week's episode that the cast and crew would be coming to Canton this week.*
>
> *Despite snowflakes in the air on this chilly Monday morning in February, a collection of housewives, retirees, and a few*

gentlemen with the day off gathered outside the radio station to cheer on the arrival of their favorite sleuthing siblings. However, many went home disappointed when the cast, running late for their recording session, sped by the assembled crowd without taking time for more than a wave. Mabel Shoemaker, our mayor's wife, who had been there for an hour in the freezing temperature, is quoted as saying, "Well that was a fine how-do-you-do! After all I'd heard about how down-to-earth Mr. Reynolds and Mrs. Gardiner are, I was highly disappointed to have been brushed aside, and I daresay I'm not the only one."

Though the fans were prepared to wait until the recording session was over to meet the stars, a studio executive soon came out and dispersed the crowd. When asked if they intended to attend the live listening event this coming Friday, several of the fans reported that they were no longer certain if they wanted to purchase tickets to the event, after such a cool reception on that snowy winter morning.

"Wow." Jeff frowned, leaning back against the couch. "That's not what I expected. Were they in a genuine hurry, do you think, or were they just being stuck-up radio stars, like the mayor's wife said?"

Tracy shook her head. "I don't think it's either of those," she said. "I think we might just have stumbled across another clue."

❖ Chapter Seven ❖

Pearl wasn't all that cold, standing outside in the thirty-degree morning with a few lazy snowflakes drifting down. She knew she had the baby to thank for that though. She'd been hot for the last month with this one, and she wasn't complaining about that happy side effect this time of year. She knew the same couldn't be said for the other fans of the show gathered outside the radio station's studio, including her own two children.

She bent over the pram to check yet again the blankets over Abigail and to make sure her little hat was still in place. Looking snug as a bug, Abigail smiled up at her and waved two mitten-clad hands, babbling a happy litany of "mama" and "dada" with a "papapapa" thrown in once in a while for good measure. She loved going for walks in the pram and

74

would be happy for a good while yet, as long as Pearl kept moving up and down the sidewalk with her.

Ruth, on the other hand, was clearly getting tired. She stopped their slow march with a whimper. "Mama, I hungry."

Pearl, one hand clasping Ruth's while the other pushed the pram, smiled at her. "We're going for lunch with Grandmother soon. Do you want crackers? I packed you some."

Given the way her lower lip began to poke out, crackers weren't the snack Ruth had in mind. "Cookies."

That did sound better right now than crackers, but Pearl had recently instituted a "no sweets until after lunch" rule for the both of them. "Sorry, sweetie. Not yet. We don't have any with us anyway."

Ruth's expression said that was the worst news in the history of the world—or at least in her young life. "But I tired." To punctuate the complaint, she made a show of dragging herself one more impossible step.

Pearl chuckled. "You're being such a good girl though. I appreciate it." Her praise didn't seem to penetrate Ruth's growing bad mood.

Distraction time. Abigail might get restless if they stopped, but it was a trade-off she'd have to make if she wanted to stay out here until Betty Gardiner and Heath Reynolds showed up. "Can you make it to the steps there?" There were a few benches in front of the building, but they'd long ago been claimed by a few of the oldest fans.

Probably around a hundred people had turned out, though it was hard to count given the way people milled about to keep warm. "We can sit. I brought you a new book to look at."

"Story!" Exhaustion apparently forgotten, Ruth bounced and attempted to make a dash for the concrete steps leading from the sidewalk to the building's doorway. Of course, given that her hand was trapped in Pearl's, she was mostly tugging and pulling and prancing.

"My, it's getting cold out here, isn't it?" A woman probably in her midforties clapped her gloved hands together and smiled down at Ruth. "They never seem to feel the cold at that age."

True for Ruth, anyway. Pearl smiled back. "If you ask her, she'll tell you she likes it."

"Wish I could say the same." The woman checked her watch. "They did say ten o'clock, didn't they? I'd think I was wrong about the next location if so many others weren't here."

They had said ten o'clock...and it was nearly eleven. Pearl might have doubted it at this point too, had Howard not been absolutely convinced that Canton was the next location—and if there weren't a banner strung across the radio station's building that read, "Welcome Joe & Josie." Surely they knew if they were about to host a nationally syndicated show.

Still, Pearl nodded. "I know. Makes you wonder if there are people standing outside other radio stations in other towns, doesn't it?"

The woman's eyes went wide, and she chuckled. "Gracious, I hadn't even thought of that. You know, I bet there are! They're coming though, right? I keep telling myself they'll be here any minute."

"They will be. I sure hope so, anyway." She'd already been there for an hour and a half, strolling with the girls. Howard hadn't been able to get off work, but he'd made her promise to tell him all about it. Wouldn't be much to tell at this point, unless he wanted a narration of how Ruth had entertained herself—first by jumping from parking block to parking block in the lot, one hand still in Pearl's the whole time, of course, to make it possible. Then by joining a game of hopscotch a few other children were playing— though they were bigger than she was and she had ended up in frustrated tears. Then she'd taken to counting snow-flakes. Always amusing, since she couldn't seem to remember that thirteen and fifteen existed and always started over once she got to twenty—or else jumped straight to a hundred.

The steps were wide, so Pearl could park the girls at one end without fearing they were in the way of any of the employees who came in and out of the building occasionally.

"I still can't believe they're coming here—not to St. Louis or Columbia or somewhere bigger." The woman held out her hand. "Mabel Shoemaker, by the way."

"Oh!" Pearl shook her hand. "The mayor's wife?"

Mrs. Shoemaker nodded. "I tried to convince Jim we ought to present Mr. Reynolds and Mrs. Gardiner with a key to the city or something, but he didn't seem to think that being a radio show star was reason enough for that." She shrugged. "What can I say? He's not quite the fan I am."

"My husband loves it. He's hoping to solve the mystery and get to audition in Kansas City for that guest spot." He was, in fact, convinced he knew the answer to the mystery of the missing coffee heiress already, though he said he needed just a little more information to be certain. Pearl pulled the new picture book out of her bag and handed it to Ruth. "I'm Pearl. Pearl Allen."

"Lovely to meet you, dear. You may call me Mabel. Your daughters are absolutely adorable."

"Thank you." She couldn't resist a grin at that, especially when Abigail cooed a hello to her admirer and gave her a big, two-toothed smile. "The little one is Abigail, and her big sister is Ruth—an avid reader, as you can see. As long as you don't ask her what the words are."

"And it looks like they'll soon have another little brother or sister joining them."

Pearl nodded and rubbed a hand over her stomach. Her coat wouldn't even button all the way anymore. Good thing she never got cold. "Two more months to go."

"Such precious times. Exhausting, but precious. Mine are all teenagers now. I don't know where the time went."

Pearl smiled. It was a sentiment she heard from everyone with older children, so she knew it must be true...though knowing it intellectually did little to give her more energy in the here and now. Abigail had taken to waking up in the wee hours of the morning, even though she'd been sleeping through the night for months on end before two weeks ago. And Ruth's afternoon nap was sometimes only half an hour, which didn't give Pearl nearly enough time to do all that needed to be done, much less take a nap of her own on days when she craved one rather desperately.

Mabel sighed. "You look positively spent, dear. You know, if ever you need a free afternoon, my oldest daughter babysits for all sorts of families. She's wonderful with children. And she graduated early last spring, so she has the time, after her morning college classes. Let me give you our number."

"Oh. Thanks." Pearl doubted they would really want to pay for a babysitter. Mother watched the girls now and then, and Opal was happy to do it when she wasn't in school. Or out on a date. Or busy with friends.

Come to think of it, having someone else on the list could be helpful, at least for special occasions. Mabel handed her a slip of paper with her phone number on it, along with Izzy—babysitter, and Pearl smiled her appreciation and slid it into her bag. "Is she booked for Friday night? Howard and I were hoping to go to the listening event, but my sister hasn't answered me yet as to whether she can help out." *And her parents already had plans.*

"I'm not sure, but she'll be home around two this afternoon if you want to give her a call."

"Thanks. I might do that." *She couldn't imagine paying for a sitter just so she could take a nap or steal an hour to herself in an afternoon, but for an evening out with Howard, the expense could be worth it.*

Commotion from the crowd grabbed their attention before more could be said on the subject, and Pearl spun in time to see a sleek blue Cadillac pulling up to the curb amidst shouts from the crowd.

"They're here!"

"It's them!"

"Finally!"

"Oh! I can hardly believe it." *Mabel reached out to give Pearl's arm an excited squeeze.* "Can you believe it?"

"I can't! It's so exciting." *The crowd had surged toward the car but, when the door opened, parted to make a path along the sidewalk. Pearl made sure the pram was secure and* that Ruth was still happy with her book and then went up on her toes to try to catch a glimpse of the actors.

She saw a flash of blond waves that must be Betty Gardiner. A moment later, a bit of her face was visible too—bright red lips turned up in a smile that looked far more strained than in any of the magazines or posters Pearl had seen.

Three men were with her. Which one was Heath? The tall fellow with the long, amiable-looking face? The shorter one with the square jaw? The redhead in the fedora? "Do you know which one is Heath Reynolds?" she asked Mabel. Maybe being wife of the mayor got her some inside information.

Mabel shook her head exuberantly, lifting an arm to wave to the approaching envoy. "No idea. But let's see if we can convince them to stop if I play the 'wife of the mayor' card." She chuckled as she said it, making it clear it wasn't a card she played often.

The four guests hurried up the sidewalk, not taking time to speak to any in the crowd who shouted their names and cheered for them. They were over an hour late, but even so, it seemed odd that they ignored everyone instead of at least waving as they hurried by.

Betty and the fellow with the longer face were in the lead, which made Pearl think that he must be Heath Reynolds. Although when a few eager fans jumped in front of them, just ten feet or so before the stairs where Pearl stood, the fellow barked out, "Move aside, please." He didn't sound quite like Heath...at least not how he sounded on the radio. Close, though, so maybe the difference was thanks to the microphone and speakers.

"Mama, look at this! Mama! Lookee!" Ruth had stood up and was tugging on Pearl's hand.

Oh, bother. She glanced down at her daughter's eager face and then back up to the approaching quartet of people. Mabel waved and shouted out a "Yoo-hoo! On behalf of my husband the mayor, and the citizens of Canton—"

Heath took Betty's elbow and, jaw set, led her practically at a run toward the stairs, the two other fellows right behind.

"Mama—look!"

Pearl glanced down at her daughter just as the group reached them. They charged right past Mabel, and the sidestep that required had Heath bumping into little Ruth, who was trying to get Pearl's attention.

Pearl gasped as her little girl squealed and pitched forward, knees buckling. The book went flying, but thankfully she collided with Pearl's legs and not with the concrete steps or the metal railing. "Ruth, sweetie! Are you okay?" Pearl tried to bend down to check, but it was hard to do with her daughter's arms wrapped around her legs and her own stomach in the way.

"Oh boy." One of the other men in the group stopped, though the stars kept on going up the steps. The square-jawed one. He stooped to Ruth's level. "Sorry about that, little lady. You okay there?"

Ruth buried her face in Pearl's side and stuck a finger in her mouth, but at least she didn't cry. Her knees must not have struck the concrete, for which Pearl was grateful. She didn't have any bandages with her.

"I think she's okay," she said, smoothing Ruth's crocheted beret. "Thanks."

The fellow straightened, reached into the bag he carried, and pulled out a handful of lollipops. "These were supposed to be for the kids, but we're in such a hurry, I forgot until now. Can she have one?"

Knowing Ruth's eyes would light up, Pearl smiled. "Sure."

He handed a lollipop to Ruth and one to Pearl too, with a wink. "For the next little one," he said, with a nod at her stomach. "And if someone wanted to be our goodwill emissary—"

"George!" The other three had all reached the doors and stood there, sending scowls toward the man speaking to her.

He chuckled and held the bag of treats out to Mabel. "Here, Mrs. Mayor—if you would? On behalf of Heath and Betty. Coming!" he called to them.

"Well, I never." Mabel clutched the paper bag—from pure instinct, Pearl was sure. The way she stared after the visitors as George jogged up the steps made her think Mabel wasn't actually of a mind to do them any favors. "After we stand out here in the cold all this time, they can't even smile and wave as they rush by?"

It had been rude. "At least that George fellow was nice."

Mabel fished out a lollipop, unwrapped it, and popped it into her mouth. "I read something about how they both have a George Scott as an agent. That must be him. Well." She reached into the bag and pulled out a handful of candy. "I'll give these out, but I don't know if I care to say they're from them. Maybe they're from the mayor." She gave Pearl a conspiratorial wink.

No one was leaving, Pearl noted as she helped Ruth with the wrapper and then unwrapped her own candy. Did they all mean to stay until the recording was done and the actors came back out? How long would that be? Would they do different takes? Multiple recordings?

Pearl checked her watch. It was already ten after eleven, and Mother would expect her to arrive at the house for lunch at least fifteen minutes before it was served at noon. There was no way she could stay another hour or more. Maybe fifteen minutes. She didn't want to leave before saying goodbye to Mabel.

The lollipop worked its magic on Ruth, who bent to pick up the book that had gone flying and presented it to Pearl.

"Balloons," she said, showing Pearl the page that she must have been excited about moments before. "I like balloons."

Pearl smiled at the colorful illustration. "Those are lovely balloons. I like them too."

In the pram, Abigail clapped. "Babababa."

Pearl chuckled. "Abbie likes balloons too. Do you want to show her the picture?"

"Yeah!" Ruth turned to the pram and propped the book up so Abigail could see it. "I read to you, Abbie. Once upon a time there is a balloon."

Pearl looked around to see what progress Mabel was making. There were a few other mothers with children present, though not so many that it would take long to find them all, and half of them were in a group by the streetlamp. Mabel was already moving away from them and circling back around.

The door to the radio station opened. Pearl glanced up and saw a vaguely familiar man step outside without letting the door close behind him. "Listen up, folks!" he shouted.

The chatter from the crowd died down to a hush. Mabel returned to Pearl's side.

The man waved his hand. "Thanks to everyone for coming. Mr. Reynolds, Mrs. Gardiner, and their agent and producer sure do appreciate the support and enthusiasm. We're going to be at it the rest of the day though, so you might as well go on home. Hope to see you all at the event on Friday night!"

Mabel snorted and turned to Pearl. "I've half a mind to tell you I'll watch your angels myself if Izzy can't and not go to the party at all."

"I'm not sure I believe you," Pearl said teasingly.

Mabel laughed. "You're a smart young lady, obviously. We'll save you and your husband seats at our table. Don't forget to call Izzy."

An invitation to join the mayor and his wife? Pearl smiled. "I won't. Though we'd better get going for now. We're due at my mother's for lunch."

"And who's your mother? Do I know her?"

Quite possibly. "Vivian Wallace."

"Oh, of course! Your little sister is in my younger daughter's class." Mabel pointed to a fellow who had a notepad in his hand. "I'm going to go let the last of my irritation out in a statement for the paper. You have a good lunch, dear, and tell your mother I said hello."

"I will." Pearl ushered the girls back to their car. Not exactly how she'd envisioned the morning going, but at least she had an interesting story to tell Howard when they picked him up from work later.

Chapter Eight

Tracy was the first to arrive at the newspaper office on Thursday, which she'd expected. No one else would come in until eight thirty or nine, but she really needed some time at the scanner to finish digitizing the February 1949 papers. She hadn't had enough downtime earlier in the week. Writing the wedding articles for the online edition had taken a surprising number of hours, leaving her little for the bonus project.

For her own part, she didn't really *need* to scan things from the archives. Grandma Pearl and Grandpa Howard had kept the relevant articles with their *Windy City Gumshoes* memorabilia, and she and Jeff and Robin had read them twice now. But she'd promised to do it for Darla and the other contestants, and she didn't want to let them down and feel like she was cheating them out of information.

She doubted the articles would be very helpful anyway. They reported on the disappointment of the fans in being snubbed by the stars upon their arrival and then on Heath Reynold's disappearance two days before he was supposed to be at the live listening party Friday night. Investigators and police had swarmed the town, asking questions of anyone who might have seen him before his costar and agent reported him missing. According to those investigators, the town and outlying areas were searched high and low. All public transportation records were evaluated, but no evidence could be found of him leaving town.

They had no leads *in* the town either, aside from a few people claiming to have seen him at a hotel and restaurant. The paper had run the photo of the friendly-looking man with the longer face rather than the broader-faced one with the square jaw.

Then, nothing. The papers went silent. Apparently, all the investigators left town, and while she imagined the *Times* would have run any other articles on him that surfaced in the Associated Press, there weren't any. Not in their own archives, and not in any of the other news archives Tracy had searched over the last two days.

Which was truly bizarre. Maybe radio stars weren't quite as big a deal as movie stars were, but Tracy just couldn't imagine that one could go missing and then be utterly forgotten within a few days. Why hadn't the investigation continued? Was the mystery simply so baffling that they had nothing to go on? Or was it, perhaps, no mystery at all?

She relocked the door behind her, since she'd be alone for at least an hour, and bustled to her desk. That last thought didn't quite settle, but it was a valid one nonetheless. Because what could be a better reason for no news being run than someone deciding it wasn't, in fact, news? Maybe Heath hadn't really been missing. Maybe he'd simply shown up after a bender or something and his agent had hushed it all up. That was what celebrity agents did now and then, wasn't it? Stifle bad press?

She wasn't sure how she'd prove that, if it was the case, or why that answer would be worthy of a river cruise. But it was still worth considering. Worth investigating.

Once settled at her desk with her computer booting up, Tracy hauled the papers out of her drawer. She had been scanning entire issues, figuring they ought to be added to the digital archives while she had them out. It was taking her longer, but it made more sense in the long run.

At least the stack was considerably smaller than it had been. Even so, she felt bad for keeping everyone waiting.

Okay, so she felt bad for keeping *most* of them waiting. She still felt a little irked with Mary Jane Shoemaker, truth be told. It seemed like every time Tracy had turned around this week, the woman was somewhere nearby. Hovering. Watching. Rushing in behind her to see what she was doing.

Jeff had told her to feel flattered because, apparently, Mary Jane had decided that Tracy was her primary competition. She didn't feel flattered though. She just felt annoyed and flustered. It was no fun to feel spied on, watched constantly. Even now, when she knew for a fact she was alone in the building, she kept jerking around, expecting to see someone there. She had a perpetual tickle at the back of her neck.

"Silly," she muttered to herself as she fired up the scanner and started the laborious process of capturing each oversized page in careful detail. Still, she found herself glancing over her shoulder regularly, half expecting to see a glowering face peering in the front windows.

At 8:28, she heard the jingle of keys, and a moment later came Annette's hum followed by her friend calling out, "You here, Tracy?"

"Yep." She was on the last paper she meant to scan in, though only the second page of it. While the machine hummed, she stood and moved to greet her friend.

Annette rubbed her hands together. "Did you get it warm in here yet?"

Cold air had gushed in with Annette and gave Tracy a shiver. "Warmer than outside by far."

Annette ducked into her office to deposit her things and turn on her computer and then slipped into Tracy's spare chair with a little sigh. "I think we need space heaters today—it's *cold* out there."

"Sure is. I'm finally about done with the scanning. What's the final count on the number of requested copies?"

"Nine. Though you might as well print a couple extra in case some latecomers show up or call about it. I think I'm going to put them on the counter with a sign telling people to help themselves. I'm over having the conversation, gotta say."

"Sorry." Tracy couldn't explain why *she* felt guilty for the extra work the contest had made for Annette. It wasn't as though she'd been the one to sponsor the thing.

"No need for you to apologize. In fact, if you weren't tackling the searching and scanning, I'd be the one trying to squeeze it in. So thanks."

"Happy to help."

Annette went back to her office with a wave, and the front door opened again a moment later to admit Eric.

The tickling on Tracy's neck eased now that some other people were there, so she finished up the scanning without feeling the need to look over her shoulder. After she set the machine to printing out twelve copies of the relevant pages, Tracy sat at her desk and pulled out the notepad from her purse where she'd jotted down a few thoughts and questions that Robin had texted to her the previous night.

The first thing on her list was SongBird Studios, the recording arm of a radio station in Chicago. She'd meant to look them up before but hadn't gotten around to it, so she opened a search engine now and typed it in.

She raised her brows as she saw the results that came in. They'd released albums way into the 1950s, and the radio station itself was still one of Chicago's leading ones, from the look of it. They had an up-to-date website with some impressive graphics, an app you could download to stream the station right to your phone, and were active on all the major social media platforms.

Tracy forwarded the site to her cousin and then clicked a few of the links, impressed. The station claimed to have always brought its listeners "today's top hits," for whichever "today" they were in. They even had a "This Day in the Charts" feed that shared the top song for each week since the station first opened in 1929. Tracy smiled as she scanned the list and saw some old favorites from her own childhood and teen years.

She took a moment and did the mental math on the opening date. This would be their ninety-fifth year in operation. And if they had records of each week's top hits going back all the way to their origins, what else might they still have record of? No doubt all the shows they once aired too, especially the ones recorded in-studio. Right? That would just make sense.

Clicking on the contact page, Tracy began mentally composing what she wanted to say as the page loaded. They had a contact form she could fill in, but they also had a variety of emails listed for the various offices.

Perfect. She chose the one for media. She'd learned long ago that Tracy Doyle, columnist for the *Lewis County Times*, got responses a lot more quickly than plain old Tracy Doyle, ordinary person, ever did.

A glance at her watch told her it was nearly nine. She drafted a quick email that basically said she was researching the show *Windy City Gumshoes* and its stars for a local-interest story. This was absolutely true, since Eric had tasked her with writing an article that would run after the contest was over, sharing the results and the mystery it disclosed. She followed that up by asking if the station had any records or history about the show it could share.

She then composed a message to Darla Franklin as well, saying she had the scans ready and asking if she'd like to meet for lunch to exchange scans for wedding info.

Nine o'clock. Time to switch gears. She knew just where she wanted to switch them to. The thought of the radio station in Chicago celebrating ninety-five years had planted the idea of a centennial in her mind. That would be a fun wedding feature. Who had gotten married in Canton a hundred years ago? No one that was still alive today, of course, but it would make a fascinating feature, especially if she could find some old photos.

"Heading back down to the archives," she called to the office in general as she went.

Her phone dinged as she descended the steep stairs. She pulled it from her pocket and saw that Darla had replied to her email with a text. How about noon at Buttermilk Bakeshop?

Darla knew how to text? That was a shock, given her seeming illiteracy with all things technical. Tracy typed PERFECT in response, sent it, and then slid her phone back into her pocket and headed directly to the shelves with the oldest newspapers, the ones already in protective plastic sleeves. These were well organized, so she had only to locate the binders labeled *1924*.

She paged through them, pausing here and there to read a few paragraphs. Even weather reports from that era were written in such a beautiful style.

> *On Thursday last, as the citizens of our fair city basked in the warmth of a summer day, all were surprised by the sudden appearance of storm clouds knuckling on the horizon. Wind gusted through town, setting hats flying...*

People just didn't write that way anymore, at least not for a newspaper. Simple facts, that was what they were all taught. No flowery language. For the most part, style and voice were removed entirely. Generally speaking, Tracy didn't mind that, but it was still fun to read some of the old articles.

When she found write-ups of weddings that looked interesting, she put that binder aside. Many had no images to go along with them and were simply announcements, but a few of those would still work.

Her fingers were turning into icicles though. That was incentive enough to carry the binders upstairs with her rather than continue to huddle in the basement.

The morning flew by as she read through the wedding articles from 1924, taking copious notes and carefully removing pages now and then to scan in photographs. There had been two truly spectacular weddings, both taking place in June. One of them immediately grabbed her attention when she saw the name Shoemaker.

James Shoemaker and Mabel Squire. Wait—Mabel Shoemaker... as in, the wife of the mayor, who had complained about the "fine how-do-you-do"? Unless there was more than one Mabel Shoemaker in Canton at the time, it must be. She swiveled to her computer and did a quick search for mayors of Canton, which she knew would be on the historical society site, and verified that James "Jim" Shoemaker was indeed in office in 1949.

She wondered, as she'd done when she saw the mayor's name, whether these Shoemakers were ancestors of Mary Jane...or Mary Jane's husband? She wasn't sure whether the woman was married or not, though she'd assumed so.

The write-up of the Shoemaker/Squire wedding painted it in glowing terms as a large and extravagant event, and it was accompanied by beautiful photographs. Tracy smiled at the tiers of lace on the drop-waist gown of the bride, the ornate bouquet that trailed all the way down to the ground, and the proud look on the groom's face.

Tracy was putting everything into her filing cabinet and shrugging into her coat when her phone rang, Robin's name and face popping up on the screen. She answered with a smile. "Hey, Robin. What's up?"

"I've got some great vintage wedding dress photos for you," her cousin said. When they were comparing notes on the contest the day before, Tracy's current work project had come up. Robin had volunteered to look in her files for pictures that could supplement Tracy's features. Even if they weren't the exact dresses described in some of the articles, she imagined there were plenty out there that would be close, and visuals went a long way toward grabbing traffic in internet articles.

"That's great," Tracy said. "I'm meeting Darla Franklin for lunch at Buttermilk at noon. Can you come?"

"Absolutely. I'll see you and Darla in a few."

They said their farewells and Tracy strode through the newsroom, grabbing a set of the 1949 papers now sitting near the door with a sign. With a smile of thanks to Annette for displaying them, she pushed out into the frigid day, shivering and zipping her coat up even though it was a short dash down the street to the bakery.

She spotted Darla hurrying inside just a few steps ahead of her. The older woman had a folder in her hands, its thickness promising. Tracy looked forward to thumbing through it all.

First things first though. They waited a few minutes for Robin to join them, and then they got in line and ordered their sandwiches and drinks before claiming a bistro table by the window.

"Sorry it took me so long to get all this finished," Tracy said as they sat. She slid the thick stack of copies across to Darla. "I was doing it in my off-hours, and there just weren't enough of them."

"Oh, that's fine. It took me a little while to put this together for you too." Darla set the chunky file on the table between them. "I couldn't resist adding some commentary here and there. Did you want me to give you the tour, or do you want to look at it when you get back to work?"

"Tour!" Robin said. "I want to hear it too. If you don't mind."

"Are you kidding?" Darla opened the folder with a flourish. "This is a stroll down memory lane. I started with the couples who are still alive—and together. Some of them I had a hand in directly, and then there are some who are friends or acquaintances. Up until the 1980s, I kept a record of weddings in town and sent cards on the anniversaries. That's how I built my business. Folks then recommended me to their friends or, eventually, their own children. It matters, you know. When you show you care."

Tracy nodded at that oft-overlooked wisdom. She'd certainly never heard of a dressmaker doing something like that, but she knew it would have gotten *her* attention.

"It eventually got too time-consuming to keep up with all the records. I certainly didn't want to send cards to couples who had just gotten divorced or if one of them had died." Darla shook her head, a bit of the light dimming in her eyes. "So much of that—both of those. But anyway, I built friendships with folks who are now some of the oldest couples in town. The first page here is a list."

Tracy leaned forward to read through the names, smiling first at the pretty floral letterhead that said *Darling Darla Designs* at the top and then all the more at the first couple on the list: Darla Dorsey and Albert Franklin. "You and your husband have been married sixty years!"

Darla nodded. "Next week, anyway. Valentine's Day."

"No kidding! That's when Jeff and I got married too. Though a few years after you," she added with a chuckle. "It'll be our thirty-second."

"Oh, congratulations! And how wonderful. I always love meeting couples who share our anniversary. There are plenty of them, right?"

Tracy laughed. "No shortage. Makes it easy to remember."

"We have another set of friends who share the day too, nine years behind us. We plan on sitting together at the Swingin' Gala and calling it 'the Anniversary Table.' You and your husband ought to join us, if you plan on attending."

"Absolutely," Tracy said. "Thank you. We'd love to join your table."

"I've got the cutest dress." Darla pulled out her phone and muttered under her breath as she swiped this way and that, clearly hitting a few wrong buttons. "This thing… My daughter insists I learn how to use it. She taught me the text message nonsense. Mostly. But where do the photos hide?" Finally, her eyes lit up. "Ah-ha! Here they are. The gallery. What do you think?"

Tracy and Robin both leaned over to look at the photo on the phone. Tracy didn't need to feign her enthusiasm for the flapper-style dress in beaded red fabric. Darla was wearing it, posing with a grin. "That's gorgeous," Tracy said. "I'm guessing you didn't order it from Amazon."

"Perish the thought." Darla sniffed in disdain, though she ruined it with a giggle. "They have some pretty ones, I grant you that, but I've seen a few, and up close they look like costumes. I wanted a real *dress*. So my daughter and I whipped this up. Do either of you need one?"

Robin shook her head. "Not me. I already took a fabulous vintage dress off my racks. Honestly, I was relieved to have an excuse to keep it for myself!" She showed them a photo on her phone.

And of course the vintage gown was fabulous, even just on the hanger.

Darla smiled. "You'll do our table proud, for sure. What about you, Tracy?"

"Truth be told, I have one in my Amazon cart. Blue with black beading." She figured it would be a bit chintzy, but it was only for one night, and the price was good.

Darla, however, made a tsking sound and shook her head. "No, no, dear, that won't do at all. You swing by the shop one day this week. We started a dress for my daughter, but she ended up with other plans. You're about her size, I think. We can get it fitted for you in two shakes of a lamb's tail." With a wink, she added, "We'll match the online price too. Otherwise, it wouldn't be put to use, and that would be a shame."

Tracy almost pointed out that Darla's daughter could save it for next year's gala, but why look a gift horse in the mouth? "That sounds awesome, Darla. Thank you. And I can't wait to see your shop."

Their food arrived, and they ate while Darla talked through the highlights of the folder. She was clearly delighted at getting to revisit some of her past creations, including a "gaudy monstrosity that I *tried* to talk her out of" for Mary Jane Hines—now Shoe-maker—in 1974.

Tracy laughed, knowing that her own dream gown hadn't exactly aged well, as evidenced by Sara's reaction when Tracy offered it for her use. She'd known full well that the puffed sleeves and lace turtleneck weren't her daughter's style. But what could she say? It was the height of fashion in 1992.

By the time Tracy and Robin had said goodbye to Darla and stepped back into the cold air, Tracy was in a great mood, knowing that the folder she carried had enough information in it to see her through the rest of the month and plenty to keep in the bank for next year if Eric decided to make it a tradition.

"Wait a moment, and I'll grab the photos I've found," Robin said. Her car was parked just outside the bakery, and it only took a moment for her to hand a thick envelope to Tracy. "There you go. I'll keep hunting and see what else I can find."

"You're the best. Thanks, Robin."

"No problem. Can't wait to see your articles."

Tracy walked back to the office, the cold making her hustle. Her mind drifted over her next potential articles. She even considered running a feature on Mary Jane Shoemaker and her husband. Maybe that would convince the woman that Tracy had no ill will toward her. And besides, this year would mark their fiftieth anniversary. That deserved some celebration.

It was really no wonder the woman had set her sights on that river cruise.

Her smile froze on her lips when she swung through the door and saw Eric, Annette, Bethany, Edmund, and Nick all in a cluster, with frowns on their faces.

Eric looked up when she came in, and waved to her. "Tracy, good. Come over here."

"Sure. What's up?" She didn't bother depositing her things at her desk, given the sober expressions on her colleagues' faces.

"I wish I knew. Any idea why WRMC Radio out of Chicago would be accusing us of libel?"

Chapter Nine

*T*racy stood beside Eric on the sidewalk at Culver-Stockton College, her eyes scanning the familiar buildings and trees and paths for an even more familiar face. Jeff had said he'd meet them in front of his building and take them to Ken's office.

Her email to the radio station that morning must have triggered the response that had Eric and everyone else at the paper so upset. She just didn't know *why*. After explaining to them that she'd sent an email asking about the history of the show, Eric had declared that they needed to talk to whoever was in charge of this contest—*now*.

It wasn't as though the libel threat could possibly hold any *real* danger to the paper. The *Lewis County Times* hadn't made a single mention of WRMC Radio Chicago to date. But someone from the radio station had emailed each and every address at the *Times* with the same dire warning—call off the contest and cease-and-desist all mention of *Windy City Gumshoes* and its former affiliation with SongBird Records, or face legal consequences.

Tracy sneaked a look at Eric. She knew he didn't take the word "libel" lightly. A suit like that could ruin them, even if they weren't guilty of it and it ended up being tossed out of court. As precarious a position as the paper had been in these past few years, just a whiff of scandal could spell the end.

He hadn't called Doug yet, though he said he meant to after he'd spoken with Ken. First he wanted to know *why* this contest would have the Chicago station up in legal arms.

They wouldn't be threatening libel unless there was some dirt—the kind that would defame somebody—that they expected to be dragged up by this contest.

And of course that was enough to make any good reporter sit up and take notice.

"There's Jeff." She nodded toward the building that housed the history department. Jeff must have spotted them, because he jogged down the steps and their way in the next moment.

Eric had a hand stretched out, ready to shake, by the time the distance between them closed up. "Thanks for meeting us here, Jeff, and for calling Ken for us. I couldn't get through to him."

"Yeah, he only checks his official voice mail once a week or so. Most of what he gets on that line are song requests for the next week's show. But I have his cell number." After shaking Eric's hand in greeting and giving Tracy a hug, Jeff indicated they ought to continue on the path deeper into campus. "He seemed pretty surprised when I said you'd gotten a threat from Chicago."

Eric snorted what might have been a laugh. "I know the feeling."

Tracy matched her stride to Jeff's, unable to stop the swell of guilt that wanted to spill out, though she bit her lip against it. She'd already apologized for the email that had triggered this response, even though she couldn't have known it would be received like this and Eric and Annette had both assured her that she'd done absolutely nothing wrong. She still felt responsible for what could well turn into a crisis if they didn't nip it in the bud right away.

A few minutes later Jeff led them into the building that housed the journalism department and up to the small office where Ken sat behind an old metal desk that looked like it had come from a school surplus sale. He stood before they could even knock on his door, a warm smile making lines fan out from his eyes. "Hey, folks, come on in. I grabbed a few folding chairs—sorry I don't have more. I don't usually have many people in here."

Jeff had told Tracy that Ken only taught one class a semester in broadcast journalism, just enough to keep him on the roster. His main focus was the radio programs he ran.

Jeff stalled in the hallway. "I actually can't stay. I have a two o'clock class. If you're still on campus in an hour, honey, let me know, and I'll come find you again."

Tracy nodded. "Thanks for showing us where to go."

"No problem." He gave her a quick kiss on the cheek, lifted his hand in a farewell wave to Ken and Eric, and then strode back the way they'd come.

Tracy followed Eric into the tiny office and took one of the folding chairs across the desk from Ken, who sat again too. His jovial expression faded into one of concern as he looked from Tracy to Eric and back again. "Jeff mentioned an alarming email that had to do with the *Turn Back the Dial* contest?"

Eric brought him up to speed as succinctly as possible. Tracy watched Ken's face, looking for some click of knowledge or realization, but his confusion mounted with each addition. By the time Eric finished, Ken was shaking his head.

"That just doesn't make any sense." He leaned back in his chair, running a hand through his silver hair. "This isn't a story about anything shady or questionable. There are no characters to be defamed or names to be dragged through the mud. It's inspirational."

She suspected as much, given the contest, but then why was WRMC afraid of it? "It seems like someone at the radio station believes otherwise."

"Then they must know something I don't." Ken shrugged and leaned forward again. "Honestly, I only know what was sent to me by the sponsor. I did some digging to verify everything they told me—and I can promise you it's all true—but I didn't have time to go any deeper."

"What can you tell us about the sponsor?" Eric had his phone out, open to a note-taking app. "Private individual? Organization?"

"Ah." Another shrug, combined this time with a sheepish look. "I have no idea. A package was delivered to me with all the information, including the two pre-paid tickets for the cruise and a note saying the cruise line had agreed to make them redeemable any time this year. I didn't believe it, but when I called them, they verified it was true. They wouldn't divulge who had purchased them though."

"So we have an anonymous benefactor sponsoring the contest. This person also gave you the details of the mystery of Heath Reynold's disappearance, right?"

Ken nodded. "And the records of the last episodes of *Windy City Gumshoes*. Which is good, because let me tell you, those things are hard to come by. Since then I've been scouring all my usual sources for earlier episodes, and there just aren't that many in circulation."

"Is that unusual for something of that age?" Eric asked.

"For one of the hundreds of radio shows of the 1940s? No. For the top mystery show for three years running? Yes. Even that came as a surprise to me, though. I've done quite a bit of research into these radio dramas and never come across a mention of *Windy City Gumshoes* until now." Ken lifted his hands, palms up, in a helpless gesture. "If it didn't sound so far-fetched, I'd say someone buried it. Pulled everything from the shelves and encouraged it to die a silent death. But that's probably me being dramatic."

"Wait," Tracy said. "So you don't actually have the answer to that part of the contest then? You don't know why the show disappeared so suddenly?"

"I don't," Ken admitted. "I'm assuming that when it's time, the sponsor will show up and let me know whose guesses go into the hopper for the drawing."

He sighed and settled back in his chair again. "The sad truth is that radio shows like this one did essentially vanish. Between 1945 and 1950, television went from being in the homes of about 5,000 wealthy Americans to being in the homes of half the families in the country. That's huge growth. No one wanted to just listen to the radio anymore. They wanted to *watch*."

Tracy nodded. That certainly jibed with her own experience. She'd grown up listening to the radio for music, but for shows, she turned to TV. "Some radio shows persisted though, didn't they? Like *Gunsmoke*?"

"Sure, there were a few exceptions," Ken said. "But even those eventually phased into television. The problem is, radio stars only needed to *sound* good. But for television, they had to *look* right too. There were plenty of times the voice actors couldn't transition successfully to the screen."

"Do you think that's what happened to *Windy City Gumshoes*?" Tracy asked. "That they tried to turn it into a television show and the actors couldn't do it for some reason?"

"I have no idea. All I can tell you is that it *didn't* make the transition. I don't know if it's a matter of the actors not looking the part, or if they just didn't get picked up, but I'd be surprised if they didn't get some offers. That popular of a show would be sitting in prime position for a small screen gig."

"Interesting." Eric's tone of voice said it *was*, he just didn't know what to do with it yet. "Maybe someone involved in the show was also involved in a scandal. Maybe that's what got the whole program canceled. Buried, like you said. Could be why the radio station is still upset about it, if it would negatively impact the family of that someone."

Ken granted the possibility with a tilt of his head, but he didn't look convinced. "I don't know much about everyone at the studio at that time, of course. But I can tell you with complete certainty that neither Heath Reynolds nor Betty Gardiner were involved in any kind of scandal."

"I won't ask you to divulge what happened to Heath," Tracy said, knowing he wouldn't anyway—or that if he did, she'd have to recuse herself from the contest. "But can you tell me what happened to Betty without giving away something I shouldn't know?"

Ken chuckled. "No big secret. She had her first child in 1950 and five more by 1960. She simply retired from acting and raised her family. I believe they ended up moving to Ohio for her husband's job."

Tracy looked to Eric. "Can you think of anything else to ask?"

Eric pursed his lips and tapped a finger against the side of his phone. "Not offhand. If you have no idea who's sponsoring the contest or what sort of defamation WRMC would want kept quiet, then I guess that's it. Thanks for your time, Ken."

"Sure. If I think of anything else, I'll let you know." He stood and shook Tracy's hand first and then Eric's. "Sorry I couldn't be of more help."

"Oh, you were a big help. We appreciate it." Eric smiled and nodded for Tracy to precede him out of the room. Once they were several steps along the corridor, he said quietly, "Actually, I really do think that was helpful."

"Oh?"

"It proves that whatever has that radio station up in arms isn't currently public knowledge. They want to keep it that way and are afraid this little contest will bring it to light. Which means that the truth is discoverable, if we ask the right questions."

"But if we print those answers, they'll sue us."

He waved dismissively. "They can only win a libel case if we print untruths that result in damages. We won't."

"But if they even bring a case, it could—"

"Put us on the map and sell a lot of newspapers? Exactly what I was thinking."

Tracy didn't know whether to laugh or sigh. "Be sure you run that strategy by Doug."

He chuckled. "Relax, Tracy. We're not going to make anything up or set out to ruin anyone's name. But if this feel-good contest happens to have a little exposé attached to it, I wouldn't complain."

Tracy jogged down the stairs and then braced herself for the cold air when they pushed back outside. A glance at her watch verified that it hadn't been anywhere near an hour. Jeff would still be in class.

"Oh, boy."

She looked up at the note of dread in Eric's voice and followed his gaze. She didn't need to ask what had gotten his attention. The teal coat, worn by none other than Mary Jane Shoemaker. "Is she following us?" Tracy's paranoia sounded ridiculous when she said it out loud, but why else would the woman be on campus?

She wasn't looking their way though. She stood with another woman who seemed somewhat familiar—and none too patient with Mrs. Shoemaker.

"Always possible, I guess. Know any shortcuts back to the parking lot?"

She did, but when the name that went along with the second woman's face popped into mind, she sighed. "That's Julie Missenden she's talking to—another history professor. I've met her several times at department events. Sweet lady."

"Oh, boy," Eric said again, this time angling a hard look down at her. "I'm suddenly wishing we hadn't ridden together. You're going to play hero, aren't you?"

"*We're* going to play hero." Without giving him a chance to respond, she strode toward the two women.

As she and Eric drew closer, she could make out what Mary Jane was saying. "It's hardly fair for you to hoard what you know, Julie. Or have you already told someone else? Did someone pay you?"

Mrs. Shoemaker's back was to Tracy, which meant that Julie caught sight of her first. Her eyes lit up. "Tracy Doyle! Hello!"

Tracy approached with a smile. "Hey, Julie. Hello, Mrs. Shoemaker. I'm glad I ran into you. I don't know if Annette had a chance to call you yet, but the copies of the articles pertaining to the Heath Reynolds disappearance are ready at the newspaper office. You're welcome to swing by any time and get them."

Mrs. Shoemaker, who had spun around when Tracy greeted her, glowered at her. "What are *you* doing here?"

Hmm. That made it sound like she hadn't intentionally followed them. The truth? Or a cover-up? Tracy lifted her brows. "My husband works here," she offered by way of truth that gave nothing away. "With Julie, actually. How are your classes going this semester?"

Julie gave her a grateful smile. She was a lovely woman, ten or fifteen years Tracy's senior, and always so gracious and kind and thoughtful. "Quite well, so far," she said. "I'm teaching an Ancient Greek course again this term, which is one of my favorites."

Mrs. Shoemaker made an impatient sound and stepped away. "Who else has already gotten the copies of the articles? Everyone? You probably told me last."

Tracy had to work to keep her face neutral. She probably didn't pull off pleasant, though she tried. "I'm not certain. Annette said she'd send messages this afternoon to everyone who left their number, but I doubt she's had time to do that yet."

"Well, I'd better go grab them before they're gone." She said it like she expected they had deliberately printed too few.

"We can always print more. Though speaking of too few copies, are you by chance finished with that book on fashion yet?" Tracy prayed it was amusement that colored her voice and not frustration or challenge. Because it *was* funny, really. "I was hoping to brush up on my fashion vocabulary for my columns this month. We're featuring weddings from Canton's history."

Mrs. Shoemaker lifted her nose. "That thing? I already returned it to the library."

"Perfect. I'll swing by and check it out then. Oh, by the way, I saw in my research for those features that you and your husband are celebrating your fiftieth anniversary this year. That's wonderful! Congratulations, Mrs. Shoemaker."

Mrs. Shoemaker paused, and her face softened. Gone was the look of fierce competition. "Thank you. It hasn't always been an easy time, I can tell you that."

"I'm sure it hasn't. But I'm always inspired by couples who make it so long. I'd love to talk to you and your husband for one of my features, if you have the time. Any time this month." She found she meant it even though she hadn't planned it beforehand.

The older woman's nod looked almost bashful. "That...that would be nice. Thanks. I...you have my number."

"I do, yes. I'll give you a call either tomorrow or next week. What time of day is better for you? Morning? Afternoon?"

"Afternoon, if you want to talk to Pat too. We'll look forward to it." She took another step away and then added, "Have a good weekend, Mrs. Doyle. You too, Julie."

Julie's sigh whooshed out the moment Mrs. Shoemaker was out of earshot. "Thanks for that, Tracy."

"Sure. I only met her this week, but you looked like you needed some backup."

Julie laughed. "Yeah. It seems this contest is bringing out the worst in some people." She shook her head and then checked her watch. "Oh, phooey. I'm running late now. I have a student meeting. Thanks again, Tracy."

"You're welcome. Have a great weekend." She waved as the woman took off at a near-jog toward the history department building. Clearly Julie knew about the contest too and was apparently putting her history and perhaps research skills to use, given Mary Jane Shoemaker's accusations.

"Man. There is some stiff competition for this contest," she muttered, more to herself than to Eric.

Her boss chuckled and nodded toward the parking lot. "You can bemoan your chances once we're out of the cold. Come on. I need to get back to the office and call Doug."

Chapter Ten

Tracy held her phone in her hand on Saturday morning but just stared at it rather than dialing the contact she had pulled up. Amy's face smiled at her from the screen.

Beside her lay the show script that had been in Grandma's attic. She'd read through it and decided it didn't have any clues in it, but she'd woken up this morning thinking about it and so had looked it over again.

Jeff was out for a jog, despite the frigid temperature, and Tracy needed to talk through her thoughts with *someone*, given that Sadie only thumped her tail in response to anything Tracy said. Robin was the logical one, but she would be gone all day with her teenage son, Kai.

She'd talked to her sister on Thursday, briefly. Enough to tell her about the craziness that had hit that week. Or the nutshell version anyway. Amy had been interested but distracted. She had errands to run for the kids, tests to grade, and she obviously wanted to spend some time with her new husband.

When Tracy had asked what Amy's weekend plans were, it had sounded like she and Miles were both booked solid and trying to carve out some intentional downtime to spend as a family.

Understandable. All of it. It just left Tracy uncertain as to whether she ought to call Amy now or respect the need to settle into her new family. Neither felt right. She didn't want to basically yell out, "Pay attention to me!" when Amy had so much going on. But she also didn't want to relegate herself to the sidelines and slowly drift away from her sister.

There had to be a middle ground. A healthy path forward. She just didn't know if that involved hitting the green phone icon now or not.

"This is silly," she muttered to herself. Amy was her sister. They'd already weathered plenty of big life changes together. And heaven knew Tracy hadn't given it too much thought when *she* was the one with the new husband and then kids taking up her time. She'd always been glad to hear from Amy. And when her sister decided to foster Jana and Matt, it hadn't changed their relationship, had it?

Her thumb hovered a moment over the green phone icon and then moved to the right and tapped the blue message button instead.

A simple solution. A text message wouldn't significantly interrupt Amy's day if she was busy, and it would lob the metaphorical ball into her court. HEY, SIS. I HAVE A COUPLE RANDOM THOUGHTS TO RUN BY YOU ABOUT THIS CONTEST STUFF. NO RUSH, BUT CALL WHEN YOU HAVE A FEW SPARE MINUTES.

Good enough. She sent the message and then turned back to the script.

The episode title was on the cover page, and she stared at it for a long moment before saying it out loud. "'The Case of the Other Joe.'" She'd printed out the episode list from a vintage radio show website, but this one wasn't on it. What did that mean? That it was unproduced? Or that the list she'd found wasn't accurate?

And neither she nor Robin had any idea as to why her grandparents had it. Had they bought it? She didn't know how much a radio script might have cost back in the day, but she couldn't imagine her thrifty grandparents forking over much hard-earned cash for something like that. The magazines and records, sure. Entertainment always ranked as things people spent money on. But a script was purely a collectible. A person wouldn't just sit around and read it for fun.

Of course, she assumed that the script had come into her grandparents' possession in the same era as the magazines and records they'd found, based solely on it being with them. But that wasn't necessarily the case. She could well imagine Grandpa Howard coming across it at a yard sale and picking it up for a few cents, adding it to their collection for the nostalgia of it all.

What got her, though, was that she was pretty sure the notes in the margins were in Grandpa's handwriting. She'd even pulled some correspondence from the attic earlier in the day to compare. She was no expert, but some of the distinctive letters looked the same.

Her phone rang, Amy's image popping up on the screen again. Tracy smiled and swiped to accept the call. "Hey, that was fast."

"Happy for a distraction from laundry. Do you have any idea how many clothes six people can go through in a week? I may have to start doing a load every day. My once-a-week schedule isn't going to cut it anymore."

Tracy chuckled. "I've never had to do laundry for that many people regularly. You could make the kids do their own."

"Hmm." The sound of a dryer door shutting came over the line and then the whir of the machine starting. A moment later, those background sounds faded away, presumably when Amy stepped out of the room. "Something to consider, though I don't think I'll throw that on them quite yet. We have enough adjustments to work through right now."

"I bet. How are the kids doing after their first full week as a family?"

"Depends on the minute." Amy chuckled, but it sounded tired. "Most minutes, all is well. For instance, this minute, they're all playing a video game together and having a blast. Other minutes, it's like a war zone in here, and you never know who's going to be on whose side. Girls against boys? Blood siblings against blood siblings? Last night they surprised me. They were arguing about something, and it was Jana and Colton against Matt and Natalie."

Tracy snorted a laugh. "Let's take that as a sign that they're forming new bonds. Surely you remember how *we* used to argue."

"I don't know what you're talking about," Amy said, her haughty tone not quite covering her amusement. "We were little angels, and I would *never* stoop to picking fights over nothing and blaming you, so that you got in trouble and I could then have access to whatever it was you'd been playing with that I wanted."

"Brat." Tracy's laugh was full that time and eased some of the tension inside. "I still can't believe I somehow got in trouble when *you* threw something at my head."

Amy laughed too and then let out a whoosh of breath, like she'd just sat down. "Anyway. Contest stuff? What's up?"

"That's what I'm trying to figure out." Tracy flipped to the third page of the script, where Grandpa—or someone who wrote very similarly—had jotted a note in the margin beside a line attributed to "Mike Hardy." The note said, *In a thoughtful tone of voice, not too sad.* "Grandma Pearl and Grandpa Howard had a box of memorabilia in the attic for the *Windy City* show, and there was a script in there."

"A script."

"You know, like a screenplay. Only, well, not for the screen. Like a play script though. All the parts written out and a few directorial notes."

"Interesting. Why would they have had that?"

"That's our question too. Robin didn't have any ideas. I figured they just came across it at some point and added it to the collection, only... There are notes in the margins, and it looks like Grandpa's handwriting."

"Huh. What kind of notes?"

"On how certain lines should be delivered. They're all around the dialogue for one character in particular. Mike Hardy."

"Maybe Grandpa was going to audition for the part." Amy said it with an amused laugh, not sounding as though she thought it a viable explanation.

But Tracy frowned down at the script. "You know...you could be right. I'd forgotten about this, but there was an announcement at the end of that first episode we listened to, saying that a fan would be given a role in the episode recorded in Kansas City. That auditions would be held the week before they recorded."

"But *Grandpa?*" Amy hummed. "He never showed any interest in acting, did he? I don't remember him ever doing community theater or even taking a speaking role in a Christmas program at church."

"Though he always managed to upstage everyone else without saying a word," Tracy said, remembering one particular program when she was in middle school. Grandpa had, as usual, been playing a shepherd—silent, meant to be background. But he'd somehow managed to find a live lamb to bring with him, though all the other animals in the play were stuffed, and he ended up chasing it around the sanctuary, greatly entertaining the congregation.

"He was such a ham sometimes," Amy agreed with a laugh. "Still. I don't think he ever had any dreams of stardom."

"Not that I remember either. But this would have been in 1949—a long time before we knew him. What if he auditioned? If he didn't get the part, that could have put the kibosh on any dreams he'd had."

"I guess," Amy said, though she sounded dubious. "I don't know. It's just funny to think about Grandpa harboring that sort of secret ambition. He worked at the same factory all his life."

He had, until the day he retired in 1975, having put in his thirty years. Then he'd taken to trolling yard sales on the weekends. The man had more toasters than anyone could ever need.

"He was creative though," Tracy said. "Remember all his lamps?" He'd had a rather impressive collection of oil lamps that he'd repurposed for electricity, filling the oil wells with colored marbles. She and Amy each had one he'd made for them when they were girls, with their preferred marble colors inside.

"And the stained glass phase," Amy added.

Tracy had nearly forgotten about that. Another of his retirement projects had been learning how to make stained glass ornaments and a few lampshades. She still had the star ornament he'd made for her. "He was pretty good at that."

"He was. But I still think it's telling that he didn't take up community theater or something after he retired. Maybe those aren't his notes on the script."

"Maybe." She was pretty sure they were, but making notes didn't mean he'd ever actually auditioned. It could have just been something he considered, even prepared for. Surely if he'd spent a few days in Kansas City reading for the part, it would have been a story they told at some point over the years. Wouldn't it?

"Maybe he got it at a yard sale," Amy suggested, echoing Tracy's first thought. "He found all sorts of weird stuff over the years."

She couldn't argue with that. "True."

"You're not convinced."

Tracy shrugged even though Amy obviously couldn't see it. "It really looks like his handwriting."

"Then maybe you're right. Maybe he considered auditioning. Could have seemed like a once-in-a-lifetime chance to do something new and interesting, right? And meet the stars of a show he liked. Guess he wouldn't have had to have any long-lasting love of acting to consider a one-time thing."

"Maybe. Anyway, that was all I wanted. Just trying to make sense of this."

"You're not turning me back over to Laundry Mountain already, are you? Surely you have more stories about that Mary Jane lady or libel threats to regale me with."

Tracy laughed. "Doug agreed with Eric's plan on the libel stuff—which is to say, don't libel, but don't get scared off by threats that are based on absolutely nothing. And I called the Shoemakers yesterday afternoon, actually, and had a surprisingly good chat with them."

"Figure out why she's been such a nuisance about the contest stuff?"

Tracy woke her laptop up and opened the email that had come in from Mary Jane's daughter last night. She'd sent along a dozen images of the Shoemakers over the years, and in all of them, the couple was smiling. Laughing. Happy. "You know, I honestly think she just wanted to surprise her husband with a trip. He's apparently still working the night shift at the railroad, despite being seventy. I got the impression that they took a hard financial hit a while back. I doubt a river cruise is something they'd be able to afford."

"That's no excuse for being nasty."

"Agreed. But sometimes overexcitement makes people do strange things." She sighed. "We had a pleasant conversation, though Mary Jane was still argumentative in odd places. Like it's just part of how she communicates."

"I've met some people like that over the years. I sure hope her husband is easygoing."

"He argued back. But it sounded…comfortable. No heat in it. Almost teasing."

"I guess that's good." Raised voices sounded in the background, and Amy said, "Oh boy. Sounds like someone's not happy with the results of the latest round of the game. I better go play referee."

"Have fun. See you tomorrow."

They said goodbye, and Tracy set her phone on the table with a deep breath. She scrolled through the Shoemaker photos again, choosing a couple that she would use in her article about them, and debated what day she wanted to run it. She had several contenders for the Valentine's Day edition, which would be in the weekly printed paper, and she'd have to get her final choice to Annette on Tuesday. The Shoemakers? The Franklins? At first she considered choosing one from a hundred years ago, but would it be better to do that, or feature a couple who were still alive and well?

She pushed the script and its unanswerable questions aside and pulled up the scan of the paper from 1924 that she'd saved to her laptop. She'd already read the write-up for that Shoemaker wedding several times. She loved how happy—mischievous, even—the couple looked in their photo. Better still, when she'd talked to the living Shoemakers yesterday, Pat had verified that they were his grandparents and had said he still had the original photos from their wedding. He'd promised to dig them out and have their daughter send them to Tracy by Monday.

Maybe that was the way to go. Especially since by focusing on a couple long-gone, she wouldn't risk offending anyone still living. If she ran the article about the Franklins—Canton's current oldest couple, so far as she'd been able to dig up—she had a feeling some other long-running couples would be miffed.

She couldn't remember what page of the scan she needed, so she scrolled through the pages, skimming the headlines as she went. It wouldn't hurt to have an idea of what else was going on in Canton at the time of its biggest wedding, after all.

Her gaze snagged on the obituaries when a familiar name caught her eye. Well, partly familiar. *Suzanne Reynolds.*

Reynolds? She paused and zoomed in so she could read it.

Suzanne Reynolds, 78, passed away on Thursday, leaving behind her two grown children, Weiland "Way" Reynolds and Lucy Reynolds Folmer, and three grandchildren, Jill, Henry, and Thomas Folmer. Originally from Chicago, Suzanne joined the Canton community ten years ago, when she moved here to live with her daughter.

Interesting. Or maybe not. Tracy read the rest of the article, but aside from the Chicago connection, there was nothing to make her think this Reynolds was any relation to Heath Reynolds.

Although, Way Reynolds…that rang a bell. Didn't Grandpa have a friend named Way?

She tried to recall. She was pretty sure there'd been a Way in his large group of friends, but she couldn't remember what his last name was. Not unthinkable that it would be Reynolds, of course. Canton wasn't that big a town, so chances were good that her grandparents had known this family.

And the last name wasn't an odd one, to be present both here and in Chicago. Even so, she got her notebook and pen out, ready to jot it down.

The sound of footsteps on the porch drew her gaze up and had her turning in her chair to smile as Jeff came inside, cheeks and nose red. "Hey, crazy man. How was the run?"

"New rule," he said, pulling off his knit hat. "No running outside when it's below twenty degrees. That was not pleasant."

"I told you so," she said, laughing.

Naturally, he punished her for that remark by coming over and burying his ice cube of a nose in her neck. She squealed and tried to retreat without falling off her chair. Her pen went flying.

Jeff laughed and pulled away. "I'm going to go thaw out in a nice hot shower."

"Smart. I'm going to…" What had she been about to do?

"Decide where you'd like to go for dinner on our anniversary? We need to decide so we can get reservations."

That sounded more pleasant than working on a Saturday morning. "Good call. I'll make a short list while you're defrosting, and we can decide for sure when you come back down."

And really, she had better make a *long* list. The disadvantage of having a Valentine's Day anniversary was that getting a reservation for dinner could be challenging. She turned to her computer, tabbed to a new browser window, and got started searching.

Chapter Eleven

Pearl sat in the car's front seat beside Howard, smiling at the song Ruth sang in the back—and Abigail's attempts to sing along, though in her baby gibberish rather than words. She could have sat against the door, but today she'd opted for the middle instead so she could be closer to her husband. Partly because she liked being close enough to hold his hand and also so they could hear each other talk over Ruth's singing.

Howard had dropped her and the girls off at the grocery store while he ran to the hardware store, and then he'd circled around to pick them up. Pearl hadn't planned on shopping this afternoon, but events had conspired against her. Ruth had been playing with the canisters in the kitchen while Pearl tried to get Abigail settled for a nap, and she'd managed to spill all the flour on the floor—which hadn't exactly been pristine beforehand. Howard had given her strict instructions a month ago to ignore the dirt until the weekends, when he'd help.

She hadn't been able to ignore the flour. And the thought of walking to the grocery store to get more in the February cold had sounded miserable. Hence, the outing. She'd told herself to view it as a fun afternoon with her family instead of an inconvenience that had very nearly reduced her to tears when she'd heard the clatter and rushed out to find her dinner plans all over the floor.

Howard shot her a smile and squeezed her hand before reclaiming his fingers for the next shift of gears. "Sorry you had such a rough morning, honey."

"It's all right," she said, even though her back still ached from wiping up the flour. "That's what I get for putting off the grocery shopping so long, I suppose. I should have done it on Monday like always instead of standing outside the radio station all morning."

Howard chuckled. "Then you wouldn't have made friends with the mayor's wife—and her daughter. I don't know about you, but I'd be willing to eat bread and water for dinner tonight if it meant someone to watch these two on Friday."

At that, Pearl smiled. She'd talked to Izzy Shoemaker on the phone on Monday, and the young woman had even dropped by yesterday after her classes at the college to meet the girls. To Pearl's utter relief, both Ruth and Abigail had taken to her immediately and were excited to get to play with her on Friday evening. And Izzy had agreed to a very reasonable hourly rate too. "You're right. I'm not actually sorry I spent my Monday there."

"Frank and Ira both said they ran into the celebrities around town yesterday." Howard put his blinker on and took the next turn. "Apparently, they weren't impressed. Frank said Heath Reynolds was rude—or dismissive anyway. Refused to give them an autograph."

"That's what I heard too. People are saying that Betty Gardiner has given plenty of autographs, but not Mr. Reynolds." As it always did on this street, her gaze skimmed over the tops of the houses, looking for the church steeple that marked their next turn.

"Sure hope I have a chance to talk to them at the party on Friday. Everyone says they sound different in person. I read an article in Scientific Journal about how the microphones and radio waves pick up certain wavelengths better than others. That's why altos sound better than sopranos on the air."

Pearl considered this. She'd never considered why so many of the female vocalists who were popular were altos, but now that he pointed it out, that made sense. She could recall several sopranos who sounded a bit whiny on air when she knew they really weren't. "Never occurred to me that was because of the equipment. Interesting."

They turned at the church, and her eyes went wide. She grabbed Howard's arm. "That's their car! The one the radio cast showed up in."

"Are you sure?" He lifted his foot off the gas.

Pearl nodded. "No one else in town has a Cadillac that shade of blue. What do you think they're doing at the church?"

"I don't think they're at the church, per se." Howard kept his speed steady, if slow, as they moved past the car.

He was right. The car wasn't parked near the doors to the church, in the lot the parishioners used. It was along the curb, closer to the gated back entrance to the cemetery. "That makes even less sense. Why would any of them be visiting a grave here?" She slid along the bench to look out the passenger window.

Only one figure stood in the rambling cemetery—a man. He wore a brown trench coat and a gray fedora, and unless the perspective was playing tricks on her, it was the man she'd spoken to on Monday. "That's George. The one who gave us the lollipops."

From the back seat, Ruth said, "I want a lollipop!"

"We don't have any with us, sweetie," Pearl replied as she strained to verify the identification. She thought the man had the square jaw and shorter height of George, but with no one else around to compare him to, height was a hard thing to gauge. He stood beside a very distinctive headstone though.

The only one in the cemetery with an angel on it. As she watched, he started walking back toward the gate, head down. "Circle the block?"

Howard chuckled, but he didn't argue. Or try to tell her that she was being far too nosy for her own good, even though that was probably true. But wasn't it a little odd that one of the Windy City radio people was paying a visit to a grave here in Canton, Missouri?

Yes. Yes, it was. Or maybe not. He could be one of those people with a love of history who just liked to visit places like this and read old tombstones. She'd met a few of those before. But surely the bitter cold would dissuade anyone from coming out here if it was merely recreational.

Howard circled the block and pulled into the church lot, glancing over his shoulder after he'd parked. Abigail had dozed off, and Ruth, still humming, had picked up the book she'd brought with her and was flipping through the pages. "Want me to stay with them, or do the snooping?"

Pearl opened the door by way of answer. "I'll be back in two shakes of a lamb's tail."

The air was cold enough to take her breath away even though she'd been feeling overly warm in the car. Definitely not the sort of day when a visitor would go sightseeing. She hurried around the church and through the front gate of the cemetery, striding along the narrow paths to arrive at the angelic marker in the center of the plot.

Fresh flowers marked a little metal vase nearby. The only one that held flowers. Last week's big windstorm had no doubt snatched any others from their holders. She moved around to look at the stone, frowning at the name. Suzanne Reynolds, 1870–1924. Beloved Mother.

Reynolds. Reynolds? *That couldn't be a coincidence, could it? But she didn't know of any other families in town with that name. Not that she'd remember anyone who died when she was a child, of course, but even so.* She looked at the neighboring plots too, but there were no other Reynolds. In fact, this part of the lot seemed to be dominated by Folmers.

That name she knew. Not well, but didn't the Folmers own a farm outside town? She had a vague recollection of a Mr. Folmer dying a few years ago, and she saw a nearby stone for a William Folmer, 1890–1947. *That must be him.* Mother had been the one to mention it. Something about how with the Folmer kids all moving away there was no one now to take care of the widow. *Lucy, wasn't it?* She had some sort of health problem, but Pearl didn't remember what it was. The Folmer kids had been quite a few years ahead of her in school.

She searched a few more rows to see if there were any other Reynolds but could find no example other than the one among the Folmers. When a gust of wind inspired her to call it quits, she dashed back to the idling car. The heat inside felt positively luxurious.

"Well?"

Pearl scooted close to Howard again. "There were fresh flowers on the grave of a Suzanne Reynolds."

"Reynolds!" Howard's eyes brightened, then a moment later his brows pulled together. "But you said that was George. George Scott, right? Heath Reynolds's agent. You really think Heath would have delegated the task of bringing flowers to a relative's grave?"

"No." She frowned at the church as Howard backed out of his spot. Tried to recall the voices of the men she'd heard on Monday. The tall one with the longer face... She'd thought it remarkable at the time that he didn't sound like Heath— and apparently others had noted the same thing. Even if recording equipment changed the sound of voices a little, would it be so noticeable to everyone?

But George...what had he sounded like? She recalled the words he'd spoken, the intonation he'd used, the good humor in his tone. Her eyes went wide. "I think that wasn't George Scott at all. I think that was Heath Reynolds."

Howard shot her a dubious look. "That can't be right."

"Why not?"

"Because you said the others called him George, and he referred to the taller man as Reynolds. He's the one whose picture was in the paper with Betty Gardiner, not that other fellow."

"Well, yeah, but..." But what? Howard was right. Everyone said the tall fellow was Heath. This shorter one, George, no one talked about him at all. Which meant he was behaving as expected, just as he had on Monday. Polite, kind, nothing out of the ordinary.

She blustered out a breath. "Then I guess he is the kind of guy to send his agent to the cemetery on his behalf." Which was really a letdown. The actor and writer behind her favorite characters was supposed to better than Heath Reynolds was being. He was supposed to be thoughtful, clever, observant, and gallant.

"That's a disappointment, huh?" Howard sighed as he turned back into traffic. "Maybe I don't want to turn in my solution tomorrow and audition for that part. Half the fun would be spending time with the cast. But now..."

Pearl reached over and rested her cold fingers on his. "We don't know what the story is here. He could have had some bad news before the trip, or not be feeling well. There's no reason to give up on that dream."

"It's a silly dream anyway." Howard shrugged, studying the road instead of stealing a glance at her, like he normally would have done. "I'm no actor. I wouldn't get the part even if I did audition."

"Who's to say? Besides, you're an ace at figuring out these mysteries. I just know you've got the solution. You'd better call it in soon, or I'll do it for you."

Howard chuckled and took the final turn onto their street. "I'll call during lunch tomorrow. I took short lunches all week so I could take an extra hour tomorrow. Figured I'd come home and call from there."

"Oh, good." He didn't come home for lunch often, but once in a while he banked a little extra time on other days so he could. "I'll make some egg salad."

"Sounds good. So...what's for dinner tonight?" The sheepish look he sent her said he almost hated to ask, but his stomach growled at the same moment.

She laughed. "Chicken noodles." Much as her mouth wanted them, her back groaned at the very thought of standing over the table and rolling out the dough. But she wasn't going to complain. She'd already done enough of that when she met Howard at the door with the girls and insisted on an errand run.

"Hmm."

Her brows rose again. "What? You love chicken noodles."

"I do, but...it's a little late. Don't they need time to dry?"

"Ideally, though they're all right without it too."

"How about you save that for a day when Ruthie hasn't made it snow flour all over the floor? I could make us some grilled cheese and tomato soup tonight. You look like you could do with a few minutes stretched out on the couch."

Pearl leaned into his side, love warming her from the inside out. "You know...that sounds absolutely perfect."

Chapter Twelve

When they found out their favorite restaurants were all booked for Valentine's Day, Tracy and Jeff opted to grab some nice steaks from the butcher shop and eat in. Once they'd decided that, Tracy figured she'd go all out. Make twice-baked potatoes, a fancy dessert, the whole nine yards.

The whole nine yards would take a lot of time though. And Tracy still had too much to do for the week's articles for the website to take the entire day off.

"Half day," she said to Annette when her friend saw her at her desk and gave her the evil eye. Annette had tried to tell her yesterday that they wouldn't miss her today. That might be true, but if she didn't get tomorrow's online wedding feature done today, when would she do it?

Annette rolled her eyes. "You just can't keep some people from working."

Having daily assignments was taking more time than Tracy was used to. But she didn't want to complain about it. "Tired of me, huh?"

"You found me out."

"I'll get out of your hair as soon as I can. Promise." She delivered this with a wink. Maybe a quarter-day could even work, if she didn't get distracted by the mountain of emails she'd been wading through each day. It seemed like everyone in town wanted to bring her attention to an inspiring couple, reminisce about whichever one had been featured last time, or offer commentary on the photos and descriptions. She expected even more feedback to come in after people read today's print copy with "the Shoemaker 1924 feature," as she'd begun to call it in her mind.

It had turned into quite a fun story. The wedding itself had set the town abuzz in 1924, of course, but then Jim and Mabel had gone on to raise three kids, win the mayoral race in 1946, and remain a beloved Canton institution for decades thereafter, even after Jim retired in the sixties from his long-running stint as mayor.

This was the sort of thing she loved about small-town life. History was so closely woven with the present. A couple that had been prominent for decades still had grandchildren, great-grandchildren, and even great-great-grandchildren living in Canton today.

And, she saw as she logged into her email, it looked like every single one of them had emailed her this morning. All the subject lines were filled with happy words, smiley faces, and heart emojis, so they'd be a pleasure to go through. But still. Seriously. She had sixty unread messages already today, and at least twenty of them were from names she recognized in her research for that article.

Someone must have warned the whole family the article was coming and told them to write in with their thanks. And she had a feeling that someone had the initials MJ.

Thoughtful, on the one hand. Kind. Encouraging.

But reading through them all would take time away from the *other* research she'd been doing, for the *Turn Back the Dial* contest. Coincidence?

She shook her head and decided all emails could wait until tomorrow. Or, for that matter, maybe even next week, after the contest was over.

For now, she focused on inputting the edits to tomorrow's online article that Annette had ready for her then uploading it to the website, adding in the photos, and getting it scheduled. It really didn't take all that long. Of course, then she had to work on the next feature too, so that Annette could review it and get it back to Tracy in time for Friday's edition.

It took more willpower than she'd have thought to ignore the ever-growing emails in her inbox. She did click into a few with subject lines that seemed to demand attention. But only a few.

She squeaked a protest when her phone buzzed. She glanced at the clock on the wall. How was it eleven thirty already?

The buzzing was a text from Sara. Tracy swiped it open and then smiled when she saw the image that popped up in her messages. A gorgeous, delicious-looking raspberry cheesecake with a caption that said, Don't make dessert! Gotcha covered. Happy anniversary, Mom and Dad!

Sweet girl. Tracy was still typing in her gushing gratitude when Jeff's answer to the group text popped up. Yum! You know us well, kiddo. Thanks.

Tracy added her own thanks to the mix, smiling still more when Sara said she'd already been by the house and put it in their fridge.

Someone cleared his throat behind her, and Tracy turned to find an unfamiliar man standing there, smiling. "Hi. Tracy Doyle?"

"That's me." She set her phone down, stood, and held out her hand. Strangers didn't often seek her out at the office, so she knew her curiosity was in her voice as she said, "Can I help you with something?"

"I sure hope so. Mind if I sit?" The way the man indicated the extra chair gave her the strangest sensation of being a guest in her own space. Like this guy was used to being the one in charge.

His hair was a rosy, fair gold that looked only a few shades shy of white, and the ample freckles over his face made her think it had once been a more vibrant red. He wore a heavy coat over a classic button-down with a pair of slacks.

Tracy held out a hand toward the chair too, even though it felt redundant. "Sure, of course. How can I help you?"

"Well, I wanted to apologize."

That got her attention. Tracy eased back onto her desk chair without taking her gaze off her guest. "Okay. For…?"

"Overreacting. My name's Ronnie Paulsen."

"Paulsen." Paulsen. Why was that familiar? Her eyes went wide when it clicked. "Related to Alfie Paulsen? Of WRMC Chicago?"

His fair cheeks were flushed, though whether from the blustery weather outside or something more, she couldn't have said. "One and the same. He was my father."

"Huh." Tracy itched to pick up her pen and jot his name down, but she suspected that might make his smile go from apologetic to accusing in a hurry. "Are you affiliated with the radio station too?"

"Yes, I'm the current owner."

Tracy smiled. "Nice to meet you."

"Kind of you to say so, given the email we sent last week."

"That was you?" Tracy hadn't been exactly slouching before, but now she snapped upright.

Mr. Paulsen tilted his head. "My son, technically, but I should have stopped him before he had a chance to send it. Sorry, Ms. Doyle. He was a bit too exuberant in his eagerness to protect the station from any bad press. When I realized he had threatened libel, you can bet I gave him a talking to." He laughed, but it sounded strained to her ears. "I told him you hadn't even printed anything that mentioned us."

"True." So far. But something about this didn't feel right. Why would a father, the owner of a radio station, drive four hours from Chicago to Canton just to apologize to her on behalf of his son? "I must say, his reaction made us wonder what exactly you were trying to cover up."

The statement was designed to bait him. To see what his reaction would be.

And react he did. He drew back and frowned. Then he renewed his smile. "We're not covering anything up, Ms. Doyle."

"Tracy, please."

"Tracy. And I'm Ronnie." He smiled a little broader, opening his hands, palms up, as if to prove he wasn't hiding anything. "It's just that the whole *Windy City Gumshoes* debacle nearly bankrupted my father the first time around, and no one wants to stir up bad memories."

She didn't point out that she highly doubted there was anyone still around who *had* those memories. Better to focus on that other tidbit. "Wait. Why do you call it a debacle? And how did it nearly bankrupt your station? From what I've been able to find, it was a very successful show."

"While it ran, sure. But when the star vanished and my father was left with contracts he couldn't fulfill…" Ronnie shook his head, looking for all the world like a caring son bemoaning the near-end of his family legacy.

So why didn't she believe him? "Sorry to hear that. Seems like he pulled the company through though."

"Eventually, yes, though he ended up shutting down the recording arm. It was a sad day when SongBird Records closed its doors." He sighed and shook his head. "Or so he always said. I wasn't around at the time, of course."

"So you drove all the way to Canton to apologize on behalf of your son? You could have just sent an email. Or called, even."

"Oh, I had other business around here. Besides, one thing my father taught me was that if you offend someone, an apology is best offered in person." He leaned a little bit closer. Every line of his face spoke of concern and a deep desire to be forgiven.

But...why? They meant nothing to him. And he meant nothing to them. Their entire experience had been one short email exchange. This response was over-the-top.

"I'm sorry if my son's enthusiasm caused even a moment's distress for you or anyone else here at the *Lewis County Times*. I assure you, we do not suspect you or any of your colleagues of nefarious motives."

"'Nefarious motives'?" she echoed.

His hands came up, palms out, in a perfect gesture of innocence. "Obviously you're above dredging up seventy-five-year-old scandals just to sell a few papers."

Tracy gave him a tight-lipped smile. "Ronnie, you're the only one who's said anything about a scandal. *I* was simply researching a feel-good human-interest story."

The confusion on his face was the first emotion she'd seen from him that looked honest. "What, exactly, is feel-good about this story?"

Well, she didn't honestly know yet. Thus far all she'd managed to find of any substance was that there were other Reynolds in Canton at some point. But whether they had anything to do with *Heath* Reynolds, she couldn't say. Not for sure. Though a family connection made the most sense, if it was, as Ken promised, a feel-good story. Maybe Heath Reynolds had been related to the Reynolds in town. Maybe his vanishing from show biz had something to do with them.

But what? And how? And how did it link to the disappearance reported here in Canton and then the utter silence about it all afterward?

She wasn't about to admit her total ignorance to Ronnie Paulsen, so instead she lifted her brows and shot back, "Plenty, from where we sit. The better question is, what are you so afraid might come out?"

That pleasant mask came over his face again. "I'm not afraid of anything coming out. But given that this story is linked to my radio station, I've obviously got an interest in how it's presented."

"Uh huh." Of course he did. But why did he think it would be presented in a way that was detrimental to his station?

He cleared his throat and said, "I personally believe in the free expression of ideas. In conversation. And I think a conversation about what happened to that show could be interesting…if it was handled correctly."

Ah, now they were getting somewhere. "Let me guess. You'd like to see the article I write before it goes to print?"

The relief in his eyes was very nearly tangible. "If you're offering, that would be perfect. We could do some internal fact-checking on anything you have and flesh out your details for you."

Her request for facts and information last week had resulted in his son's accusatory email. Now he was suddenly willing? "And, presumably, you'd make sure nothing I said reflected poorly on your station."

Another of his sheepish smiles. "I admit, we'd rather have good press than bad. Is that so unthinkable?"

"Not at all." But he *expected* bad. Which meant there was something other than feel-good at work in this story, to be sure. Tracy smiled. "I'll be happy to send you my article, Ronnie. Once I've written it. But that won't be until next week, after the contest ends." After *she* knew what she meant to write.

"Yeah, about that." He made a face that bordered on pained. "A whole town full of people digging into ancient history around this… I admit, it gives me a headache just thinking about it. Even if you don't write anything negative about my station, who's to say one of the contestants won't go on social media, badmouthing us for dropping the show back in 1949?"

The thought of Darla or Mary Jane engaging in an online battle was enough to make a snort of laughter sneak out. "I would be surprised if most of the people entering this contest even have social media accounts."

"You never know."

"I guess not. But I can't help you with that. The paper isn't sponsoring this contest, and the radio station that announced it says that there's nothing but happily-ever-afters to dig up. Whatever you're afraid of, that isn't the story being told around here."

"So who is?"

"Who is what?"

He sighed out what sounded like frustration. "Who is sponsoring this contest, if not the paper? I looked into the radio station, and it's a public broadcasting channel. No way they have pockets deep enough for this."

She shook her head. "Private, anonymous sponsor. That's all anyone knows."

He straightened, like that actually told him something useful. He stood. "Well. Thank you for your time, Tracy. And I really would appreciate seeing your story before it runs."

"Sure." She'd send it to him. She wouldn't promise to incorporate his edits…but maybe they'd tell her something he didn't intend. "Safe travels back to Chicago."

"Thanks." He shook her hand and then strode away as if he couldn't wait to get on the road.

Business in the area, he said. What business? And had he seen to it already, or was that next on his agenda?

Tracy slid her phone into her purse and grabbed her coat. A dash to the door, and she peeked out the glass just in time to see him climb into a bright yellow newer-model hybrid car.

Not too many of *those* around Canton. Good. She slipped her coat on, gave him a minute to start up his engine, and watched.

"Why do I feel like you're thinking about becoming an investigative reporter for the afternoon instead of baking your potatoes?"

Tracy shot Annette a smile. "I can do both." To prove it, she darted outside and to her car just as Ronnie Paulsen pulled out onto the street, heading right.

Well, what a coincidence. Exactly the direction she needed to go too, at the time when she'd been planning to leave. She got into her car, thumbed a quick text to Robin to let her know she was chasing a lead that had to do with the radio station, and then pulled out in the same direction. She spotted the distinctive yellow four cars ahead of her. Perfect.

He wasn't behaving like he thought someone was following him and he was trying to lose the tail. No last-minute turns, no zigzagging. He used his blinker and turned a moment later into the parking lot of an old church.

Okay. Interesting. Tracy had never even been inside that building, though she remembered Grandma Pearl pointing it out as the one they'd attended when she was younger, before there was a split in the denomination and her family switched to a different church altogether. She'd driven past it countless times though, admiring the graceful steeple, the brickwork, and one of the oldest cemeteries in town.

She drove past it this time too and pulled into the parking lot of the furniture store across the street. She'd no sooner put her car into park than a return text arrived from Robin. I DON'T KNOW WHAT YOU'RE UP TO, BUT BE CAREFUL.

Tracy's lips twitched into a smile. Her cousin knew her too well. She tapped in a quick update on her visitor and where she was, chuckling when Robin replied with an even stronger demand to be careful.

She would be, of course. And was proving it by making sure someone knew where she was.

After a few minutes of sitting there feeling conspicuous and wondering if maybe Ronnie had just stopped to fiddle with his GPS or answer a phone call, his car door opened and he stepped out.

He looked around, but Tracy didn't duck out of view. Movement would catch his eye more than anything, and she highly doubted he knew what car she drove. His gaze didn't latch onto her as he walked alongside the church and let himself into the cemetery by way of the vintage-looking wrought iron gate.

Interesting. Why would a stranger from Chicago decide to take a twenty-degree stroll through an old cemetery?

Correction. He wasn't strolling. He was reading headstones, moving from one row to the next, clearly looking for something in particular. He finally paused, half-hidden behind a massive angel with the tip of one wing broken off. A moment later he returned the way he'd come, shaking his head.

Presumably he'd found what he was looking for. Not that it seemed to make him all that happy. He was back in his car a minute later and pulling out onto the street.

Tracy did the same, careful to yet again put multiple cars between them. She expected him to head for the interstate or maybe a restaurant. It was lunchtime, after all.

Instead, he turned onto a county road that led to...nowhere, really. Eventually it would hit another town, but not for miles. Mostly out that way were farms and the occasional housing development.

Why would he head that direction? Was his GPS just detouring him away from a traffic backup or something? Hers had certainly sent her on some bizarre routes now and again.

She debated for only a second before taking the same turn. There were no cars between them now, which made her antsy, but she hung back far enough that there was no way he'd be able to look in his rearview mirror and tell who she was. Far enough that she lost sight of him several times when the road twisted.

If he weren't driving such a brightly colored car, she wouldn't have noticed at all when he turned—but that spot of yellow driving down a lane off the lefthand side of the road stood out like a canary among the grays and browns on the landscape.

She had a vague sensation of having been on that lane before, but she couldn't have said when or why. The land on either side had, from the look of it, once been a farm, but it didn't appear to be an operational one now. None of the fields were plowed over, and she didn't see the usual heavy equipment or the sheds where they'd be stored for the winter if they weren't out being used to do whatever it was farm equipment did during the off-season.

But the house and surrounding yard that the lane led to was beautiful. Well kept. She spotted weeping trees that were likely ornamental cherry and would be gorgeous in a month or two, extensive gardens, benches and paths, and a trellis with some sort of now-dormant vine climbing up it.

She was almost sure she'd been there before. For some event. She had a sudden image of people all around, laughing, of twinkle lights in a summer garden, and Jeff at her side. Maybe a wedding? It looked like the sort of place that could be rented for events, or host them for family.

She didn't turn down the lane, obviously. But she did look at the name on the mailbox at the end of the long driveway. FOLMER.

Folmer. That sounded familiar. She'd just read it recently, but where? She'd read so much local history the last two weeks that she was pretty sure she'd come across every single family name ever to settle in Canton.

She tucked it into her memory and drove past the Folmer farm, choosing a driveway a half mile down the road to turn around in. The yellow car was still parked at the graceful, rambling house on the Folmer property when she drove back by.

Clearly not just a wrong turn or his own attempt to turn around. Ronnie Paulsen must know who lived there. Which meant he had some tie to Canton.

A tie that he seemed pretty eager to keep hidden.

Chapter Thirteen

*T*racy could admit it. She felt a little odd traipsing through a church cemetery that contained, so far as she knew, none of her own relatives. She was keenly aware of having no reason to be here beyond her own curiosity, and it had her checking over her shoulder and squinting to see if anyone watched *her* from behind the windows of a car parked at the furniture store.

The yellow hybrid was nowhere in sight. There'd be no mistaking that, which gave her a measure of peace.

A glance at her watch told her that the rumbles of her stomach were right on cue. It was past noon, and she was lucky Sara had provided the cheesecake. Otherwise, she'd be well on her way to woefully behind schedule. As it was, she tried not to think about it and simply lifted her scarf to cover her nose and mouth when a particularly nasty gust of wind had her huddling in her coat.

Finding the grave with the angel marker was easy enough. She read the inscription on it. *Jeremiah Smith*. Didn't ring any bells. But the whole bell choir let loose when she looked at the neighboring stones.

Folmer. Folmer, like the farm she'd seen Ronnie Paulsen visiting. Was it something as simple as him knowing the family? Coming here to pay respects and then visiting whoever was still around?

Possibly. How was she to know? She looked at the names and dates, but they didn't sound terribly familiar.

Wait. Lucy Folmer, who died in 1952. *That* name she'd read recently. And there, beside it. *Suzanne Reynolds.*

She sucked in a breath and a little bit of scarf along with it. Suzanne Reynolds, formerly of Chicago, who had two children who survived her—Weiland and Lucy Reynolds Folmer.

And there, beyond Lucy, was that other familiar name. *Weiland Reynolds*, whose stone had not only years, but dates. *April 4, 1910-September 13, 1985.*

Hold on—September 13, 1985… That was Grandpa Howard's sixty-fifth birthday. Her brows knit, long-forgotten memories sifting to the surface. In 1985 she was fifteen, far more concerned with her own life than her grandparents' friends. But she remembered helping her parents and Grandma Pearl put together a big party for Grandpa Howard's sixty-fifth. They'd rented the fire hall and invited pretty much the whole town, but Grandpa had been too upset to really enjoy it because a friend of his had died that day. Way.

Way Reynolds.

She stared at the tombstone, willing more information to appear on it. Some clue as to why Ronnie Paulsen had been standing there, in the Folmer/Reynolds section of the old cemetery.

It couldn't be coincidence. She was convinced of that now. Heath Reynolds had to be some relation to the Reynolds buried here, and one of them had married into the local Folmer family. She pulled off her gloves long enough to snap a few photos of the headstones in the area and was glad when she didn't drop her phone in the process, so quickly did her hands get cold.

Shivering, Tracy spun around, nearly jumping when she saw the figure standing against the fence on the street side. For a split second, she expected to see faded red hair and freckles on a man of average height, but no. It was a woman, and it only took her a second to recognize the face peeking out between the thick hat and the thicker scarf. Tracy smiled and lifted her hand. "Hey, Julie."

Julie Missenden lifted a hand in hello but didn't say anything that Tracy could hear. For a second Tracy debated whether she ought to go over and strike up a conversation with Jeff's colleague, but before she could decide, Julie walked away.

Not that she would have minded another chat with the woman, but she was glad not to linger outside today. Tracy hurried toward the front gate, through it, and around the corner of the church. Her ears registered the squeak of another gate, farther away, as she reached the parking lot. The cemetery had a back entrance—she'd seen it. And she had a feeling Julie had just made use of it.

Well, what did she expect? That she was the only one making these connections? Of course not. Frankly, she was surprised Mary Jane and Darla weren't at her heels too, and a half-dozen others besides.

By the time she pulled in at home and got into the house, she still wouldn't have called herself *warm*, but the worst of the chill had thawed in the heat of the car. She was suddenly glad that her afternoon involved a lot of oven work.

She ate a quick lunch, scrubbed and oiled and pierced the potatoes and got them in the oven for their first bake, and then sat down with her laptop and the photos on her phone. She sent the photos to Robin.

Her cousin's reply was quick. ARE YOU HOME? I CAN COME OVER AND SORT THROUGH IT WITH YOU. I'LL HELP YOU COOK DINNER AND VAMOOSE BEFOREHAND, PROMISE.

Well, she'd be a fool to pass that up. Tracy typed an enthusiastic agreement. While she waited for Robin to arrive, she turned back to the photos.

Suzanne Reynolds, whose obituary she'd seen in the 1924 paper. She'd died the same week that Mabel and Jim Shoemaker got married. Survived by Weiland and Lucy Folmer. Lucy, who'd died in 1952. Tracy made a note to look up that obituary when she was next in the office. But the one for Weiland Reynolds, who had died on Grandpa's birthday, she could access here and now—those papers had already been scanned and were available online. She stopped for a moment, recalling how that birthday had been the last one they celebrated for Grandpa Howard. He died the following summer of a heart attack.

She logged into the newspaper's site and did a search, finding the obituary quickly.

Weiland "Way" Reynolds, born in Chicago in 1910, died on September 13 at the age of 74 and leaves behind a community that will greatly miss his laughter, kind heart, and generous spirit. Way moved to Canton from Chicago in 1949 to care for his sister, the late Lucy Reynolds Folmer, and so loved the town that he stayed on after her death in 1952. Though Way never married or had children of his own, his countless friends and neighbors gladly claim him as their own. "Uncle Way" was famous for his portrayals of Santa Claus every

Christmas, his laughably bad bowling game, and the children's plays he wrote for area churches. Way made his living through freelance writing under a nom de plume, but even his closest friends are unaware of his pen name.

The article went on to talk a bit about Way's early life, where he attended school, and his brief service during World War II before an injury sent him home. Tracy skimmed those parts then scrolled back up to the black-and-white photo printed alongside the column.

The man in the picture reminded her in some ways of her own grandfather. Not in features but in the way he was dressed, the style of glasses he wore, the way his hair was styled. And she could definitely imagine Grandpa Howard grinning at the camera like that. This fellow was older than Grandpa had lived to be though. The photo must have been taken somewhat near his death in 1985, because he certainly looked like he was in his seventies. Hair that probably would have appeared gray even in a color photo, lines wrinkling his face, skin gone soft and sagging.

Aging skin couldn't hide his most prominent feature. A square jawline.

Tracy stared at the photo for a long minute before pulling up her saved searches for Heath Reynolds. She resized her windows so the photos were side by side.

Way definitely looked nothing like the most often used photo of Heath, the handsome fellow with the long face. But the other one, the one on only one or two sites… She glanced from one to the other and back again. There were differences. Hairline, wrinkles, and the obvious addition of nearly forty years.

But it was the same man. She had no doubt about that.

"Hello, hello!" Robin called out as she let herself in. "Man, it's cold out there!"

Tracy glanced over with a smile but waved Robin over to join her rather than commenting on the weather. "Come take a look at this. One of the lesser-used photos of Heath Reynolds and Grandpa's old friend, *Way* Reynolds."

Robin bustled to Tracy's side as she shrugged out of her coat. Her brows went up. "Whoa. Same guy. Obviously the same guy."

"Right? I don't know who the other man was, the one that most of the world seemed to think of as Heath Reynolds, but *this* was the real Heath. It has to have been."

"So his real name was actually Weiland. Same last name, from Chicago, where Heath worked and recorded the show he wrote."

"*And* he went on to earn a living as a writer using a pen name."

"Plus—and this is quite the clencher, I think," Robin said, "Heath Reynolds disappeared in Canton in 1949…and Way Reynolds moved to Canton in 1949."

They exchanged excited grins as Tracy jotted down at least half of the mystery's answer—they knew what had happened to Heath Reynolds. He simply reverted back to his birth name and moved to his sister's hometown to care for her.

"But what happened to his legacy?" Tracy asked, sobering.

Robin let out a long exhale and pulled out a chair. "Good question. We still don't know why Heath was reported as missing or why all mention of him and his show was buried."

"No, we don't. Although, given the sudden appearance in town of Ronnie Paulsen and his visit first to the Reynolds/Folmer cemetery plot and then to the Folmer farm, along with his insistence that the story would defame his company…"

Robin nodded. "We at least know what direction to look."

They knew something else too. They knew that their grandparents were fans enough of the show to have a box of collectibles related to it, and they knew that Grandpa Howard and Heath— or rather, Way—were friends. They'd bowled together every week. Tracy was pretty sure she herself had been one of the kids delighted by Uncle Way's portrayal of Santa Claus at Christmas. She'd played a part in a play he'd written for their church's children's group— something with stars as the main characters, putting on a show for Jesus's birthday.

She might never have heard of *Windy City Gumshoes* until ten days ago, but she'd known Heath Reynolds all through her childhood. He had helped *shape* her childhood, even if she hadn't realized it.

Tracy hummed and tapped a finger on her notepad. "I bet there's more information up in the attic about Way Reynolds."

Robin nodded and stood again. "I bet you're right. Bowling things or the like. Didn't they used to have yearbooks for the league? Or whatever they called them. I remember Grandpa Howard showing them to me during my very brief decision to be a professional bowler at age ten."

Tracy chuckled and stood too. "One way to find out, right?"

The oven clicked back into its heating cycle as she walked by, for which she was grateful, or she may have forgotten all about the potatoes. She checked the time left on the kitchen timer and set her cell phone's timer to match. Then she grabbed a thick sweater on her way past the coatrack and a second one for Robin to borrow.

The attic was as cold as it had been when last she was up there, though at least now there was some sunlight drifting through the window and setting the dust motes to shining. They moved slowly through the space, arms folded to preserve heat, and read the labels on the cardboard boxes that were in sight. When Tracy spotted one that said BOWLING on it, she tugged it out with a call to Robin. Though it *felt* like there was a bowling ball inside, there wasn't. Papers, booklets that looked a little like those old yearbooks, a hand towel with *300!* embroidered on it, and who knew what else beneath that stuff.

They put that one aside to take downstairs and kept searching. Any box that looked like Grandpa's memories from the fifties up until his death, they pulled out.

It took them two trips to get everything down to the warmth of the kitchen, but they were making the last trek when her phone's timer, and the kitchen one, buzzed.

A test of the potatoes told her they were cooked through, so she took them out of the oven to cool and then turned to the boxes of memories that Robin was unpacking.

In the bowling box, they found quite a few team photos, dating all the way from the early fifties, when Grandpa was still quite a young man and one of the youngest on the team. Way Reynolds was in them all, first looking to be in his forties and an exact match for those rare images of Heath, and then aging with each consecutive year, just like Grandpa did.

Robin smiled as she flipped a page. "It's interesting to watch the group grow older together, isn't it? To see new faces come in to replace ones that left. And even to watch the photos themselves change in tinting."

Tracy nodded. "Even how their team shirts evolved over the years, and the background of the bowling alley. It's like watching the twentieth century progress through one very particular lens."

The yearbooks were for the whole bowling league. Not one per year or anything, just here and there. They flipped through them, searching for familiar faces, smiling at the fun it looked like the guys had, but otherwise not spending too much time on them.

The bowling box didn't really offer much else, so Robin slid the next one forward. Tracy had grabbed it because the collection inside looked so random. All sorts of magazines and even a few pulp novels from the sixties. Why weren't those on the bookshelves in the library? The very oddity was what had grabbed her attention, and she was fairly sure her instincts had been good after a few minutes. The books all bore the same author's name—Chance McGee—and they were mysteries. She pulled out the magazines and flipped to a few marked pages, smiling when she saw the same byline for Chance McGee on an article in each one.

"Way's pen name?" Robin mused.

"Maybe. We can't know for sure, of course, unless Grandpa had a note in here somewhere. But it seems likely. Why else would he have a collection of books and articles this McGee fellow wrote yet have them in a box in the attic instead of in the library?"

Robin granted the point with a tilt of her head. "It does smack of Grandpa's sentimental but disorganized way of storing what he thought was important."

Tracy picked up one of the mystery novels. There was no time to actually read it before they had to turn their answer in to Ken, probably, but she'd skim a few chapters and see if it bore any resemblance to the *Windy City Gumshoes* episodes in style or voice. In which case she should probably pull out the oldest of the books. That would likely be closest in writing style.

Although the oldest was copyrighted 1960, which was still eleven years from the last episode of the radio show. That was a lot of time for someone's writing to grow and change.

Robin's phone chimed, and she looked at the screen with a sigh. "Uh oh. I'm being called back to the shop. And I haven't even proven myself useful with dinner yet."

Tracy laughed and made a shooing motion. "You were more than helpful with the attic stuff though. Go on. Dinner's under control. I think I'll just sit here and read a little."

Robin flashed her a smile and reached for her coat. "Let me know if it's any good."

"Will do." Tracy saw her cousin out and then settled back at the kitchen table and opened the book. She'd read the first two chapters when her phone rang, jolting her out of the story—which was quite good—and making her realize that she probably should have chosen a more comfortable chair. She shifted for the phone and winced a little at the ache the hard wooden surface brought to life in her back.

Darla Franklin's name was on the screen. Tracy answered with a smile.

"Happy anniversary to you and your husband!" Darla sang out over the line.

Tracy laughed. "Why, thank you. A very happy sixtieth to you and yours as well. Do you have big plans for the night?"

"Oh, the big-big plans include a party our kids are putting together in a couple weeks and of course the gala this weekend—

that was our gift to each other. Tonight we're just grabbing some chicken sandwiches and milkshakes. How about you?"

"Nice dinner in tonight. Steaks and twice-baked potatoes and a salad, and my darling daughter dropped off a cheesecake for us."

"Never been much of a cheesecake fan. I know, I know, no one can ever believe it." Darla chuckled. "Ice cream. That's my weakness."

"Hence the milkshakes."

"Hence the milkshakes. How's the hunt coming along? Have you turned in your answer yet?"

Had it been Mary Jane on the line, Tracy would have thought, *Ah, here's your true purpose in calling.* But with Darla, it sounded more like an afterthought. Like the anniversary wishes were the real purpose. Though maybe Tracy just wanted to give her the benefit of the doubt. "Not yet, but I'm close, I think. I found some rather useful information in my grandparents' attic."

Another laugh came across the line. "If their attic is anything like mine, it's a regular museum full of crazy history. Watch out for the pharaoh's curse, right?"

Tracy chuckled. "About the size of it. Wouldn't surprise me at this point to find an old sarcophagus up there. My grandmother did have a small Egyptian cat statue, actually. Even had a supposed-curse attached."

"Ooh, that's fascinating!"

"We're looking forward to sitting with you and your husband at the gala," Tracy said. "I've told Jeff all about you guys. And your feature will run that day in the paper too. I thought it would be fun to schedule it for the day of the party."

"Oh, aren't you the sweetest? We're looking forward to it too. But I'd better let you get back to your afternoon. Enjoy your dinner—and beware of that pharaoh's curse, now, if you find your-self up in the attic again."

"I will," Tracy replied. She shook her head as she disconnected then stared at the phone for a moment. *Pharaoh's curse.* Had it been her imagination, or had Darla said it the second time with emphasis?

And why did it sound so familiar?

Her gaze drifted back to the boxes of Grandpa's stuff, and then she shot out of her chair with a gasp. "Darla Franklin, you're too clever, aren't you?" She dashed into the living room, where all the *Windy City Gumshoes* stuff still sat under the table with the lamp and radio. After easing down to her knees, she flipped through the records, pulling out the second one in the stack. "'The Case of the Pharaoh's Curse,'" she said under her breath.

They hadn't bothered listening to these early episodes, figuring they wouldn't have anything to do with the mystery at hand. But did this one? Darla wouldn't drop a hint of a clue just to derail her, would she?

She didn't think that was the woman's style, though really, she barely knew her. But why would Darla share a clue with her? Surely her kind heart didn't go quite that far.

Tracy stood, album in hand, and moved over to the record player they'd set up. It certainly wouldn't hurt anything to listen to it.

The intro music was familiar by now, as was the tag line. *In the windy city...* As she listened, Tracy straightened up a bit and even picked out a few CDs to put on during dinner that evening.

The episode was interesting, well written, and clever. She found herself smiling several times at the wit of the characters, especially Josie, who had quite a biting tongue. No wonder Grandma Pearl had liked this show. Josie was just the kind of heroine she'd get a kick out of. The supposed pharaoh's curse that they were investigating on the behest of a museum's curator reminded her in some small ways of the story of the cat statue that had been in the attic for a hundred years that she'd mentioned to Darla.

Eventually she ran out of things to do in the living room, so she sat down on the couch to listen to the last fifteen minutes.

"We're looking for answers," Joe said from the record player, speaking to an uncooperative museum employee, "and we're going to find them. Every clue, every crumb, every thread, will lead us somewhere. One step closer to the truth. And you can bet we'll follow each one."

And they did, of course. The resolution was neat and satisfying and delivered that "Of course!" ending that made perfect sense in retrospect, even though Tracy hadn't seen every detail of it coming beforehand. She could see why her grandparents had bought this particular episode to listen to over and over again. It felt rich and exotic with its Egyptian tie-in. And had some fascinating historical tidbits about Egypt too.

But nothing in the episode seemed to have a direct link to the situation they were currently investigating. Why had Darla dropped the name like that?

Every clue, every crumb, every thread,…

Tracy's brow furrowed. That sounded familiar. But why?

She settled on the couch with the packet of 1949 articles, grateful once again that Sara had made that cheesecake. This could take some time.

Chapter Fourteen

"Oh, it's horrible—just horrible! Have you heard? Did you read the paper yet?"

"What?" Pearl hadn't so much as brought the paper inside yet. She was still in her housecoat and slippers, her hair in rollers. The morning had been one battle after another, trying to convince the girls to eat their breakfasts. Why they loved oatmeal one day and hated it the next, she couldn't begin to comprehend. "Who's this?" The voice on the phone sounded more mature than any of her friends but definitely wasn't Mother.

"Oh, how silly of me. It's Mabel. Mabel Shoemaker? We met—"

"Of course. Sorry I didn't recognize your voice, Mabel." The mayor's wife was on the phone—had called her. At nine in the morning. But why? The only thing they really had in

157

common at this point was her daughter Izzy being their new babysitter. Pearl drew in a sharp breath. "Is Izzy okay? Nothing happened to her, did it?"

"What?" Mabel sounded as baffled as Pearl had a moment before. "Oh, gracious! No, no, Izzy's fine. Sorry. It's Heath Reynolds. He's missing."

Missing? Pearl wiped a stray glob of oatmeal from the cabinet—Ruth's complaints about it had inspired Abigail to fling a spoonful across the room—and frowned at the phone's cradle, as if Mabel could see her through it. "What do you mean?"

"Exactly that! No one's seen him since yesterday morning, and apparently some sort of threat was received, though I don't know what, exactly. Betty Gardiner has been outside city hall all morning giving statements. She's completely distraught, and the town is positively overrun with investigators."

"Oh no! I assume our police are involved too then? Looking into it? Why would there be other investigators?"

"Sounds like Mrs. Gardiner and Mr. Scott called them in. I expected Chief Dorsey to be upset about that, but he seems to be taking it in stride."

Pearl had never met the chief of police, but obviously the mayor's wife had. "That's...good? I guess."

"Out of character, that's what it is. Chief Dorsey is a stickler for jurisdiction. But I guess even he realizes that with celebrity sorts, you'd better just roll with the punches, as they say."

Pearl made an agreeing noise and picked up the cradle so she could walk the steps necessary to peek into the living room. Abigail was stacking blocks, and Ruth played with the doll she'd gotten for Christmas. Their happiness could dissolve at any moment, of course, but perhaps it would hold out while she was on the phone.

"I feel so terrible," Mabel went on. "Those things I said to the reporter on Monday! I ought to have offered them more grace. They'd clearly had a long journey full of delays, and there I was, bellyaching about being kept waiting and not getting an autograph. Oh, to think that my words may have been one of the last things Mr. Reynolds read before...this."

This. *Going missing.* "Do they suspect...?" She didn't even want to breathe the word *murder*. Somehow, giving voice to such a fear made it far too real.

"I have no idea. There's certainly no crime scene, no evidence to suggest anything that bad."

"Good. I'll be praying he turns up."

They chatted a few more minutes before Mabel had to attend to something else. Just as well, since the girls were getting restless too. After saying goodbye, Pearl put the phone back, intervened before Ruth's deciding she wanted to play with Abigail's blocks could turn into a screaming match, and then hurried into a dress. She plucked the rollers from her hair and darted out to the front stoop to gather the paper.

The cold snap had vanished, and in its place a temperate breeze blew that actually made her linger outside for a moment, looking up at the clear blue sky. Funny what a difference a day could make. Yesterday she'd all but frozen in that cemetery and today...

Wait a minute. Hadn't Mabel said that Heath disappeared yesterday morning? But she'd seen that man yesterday afternoon, and even if it was George Scott and not Heath, why would Heath's agent be visiting the Reynolds family's gravesite when his good friend and client was missing?

But she believed even more today that it hadn't been George Scott at the cemetery. She'd pulled out a couple of their Windy City albums last night and listened after dinner, and she was all but certain that the voice of Joe, played by Heath Reynolds, was the same voice that had come from the square-jawed man on the steps to the radio station. Maybe he'd wanted to remain anonymous as he traveled, or perhaps he had some other reason for the trading of names. But that was Heath, she was all but certain of it. And he had most assuredly not been missing yesterday.

It took a lot of effort to bend over for the paper and then straighten up again. The way she huffed and puffed, anyone watching would have thought she was preparing to blow down the house of a few little piggies rather than execute a simple task. Smiling at the image, Pearl went back inside and settled on the couch with the newspaper.

The front page proclaimed the same news Mabel had shared, although the photograph they ran of Heath was of the taller fellow.

Doubt of her theory welled. This information had to have been provided by Betty Gardiner, George Scott, and that redheaded fellow. His friends, his colleagues. They surely knew what he looked like, so obviously her brilliant deduction was wrong.

She read through the article, her brows furrowing when she got to the quote from the lead investigator. She read it out loud. "'We're looking for answers, and we're going to find them. Every clue, every crumb, every thread, will lead us somewhere. One step closer to the truth. And you can bet we'll follow each one.'"

"Wait a minute," she mumbled, reading that line again. And the attribute—according to the paper, a fellow named Bernard McFarland had said it. He claimed he was one of Chicago's leading investigators, called in by the radio crew.

Pearl pursed her lips. One of Chicago's leading investigators had said that, all right. A fictional one, in "The Case of the Pharaoh's Curse." She'd just listened to it last night. There was no way a real investigator would use that exact same sentence, word for word, about a case involving the writer of the original lines.

Something wasn't what it seemed.

She hauled herself to her feet. "All right, girls. It's warm outside today, and we're going to the park to enjoy it before Daddy comes home for lunch."

The girls were always happy to play at the park, and given the warmth of the day, Pearl didn't mind that they had to walk, since Howard had the car. Soon enough they were outside, Abigail happy in the pram and Ruth skipping along beside her. Once at the park, Pearl pulled the baby out and let her toddle around, keeping a close eye on her lest she decide to taste the rocks or mulch. Ruth ran to join a few other kids her age who were rolling a ball around.

There was no shortage of children at the park. Plenty of other mothers had decided to take advantage of the unseasonable warmth too, just as she'd hoped. These women, who had husbands and brothers and fathers in pretty much every business in Canton, were all eager to talk about the Heath Reynolds case.

Suellen Johnson, whose husband worked at the train station, said that Gary had seen two of the radio fellows—she didn't know which two—at the depot the other night, talking in hushed tones before one of them got on a train for Chicago. Heath wasn't missing at all, she insisted. He'd just gone home.

Irene Masters shook her head. "Oh no," she insisted. "He's definitely missing. I don't know who Gary saw, but it couldn't

have been Heath. My mother was there for the actual disappearance! She waited their table at the diner for breakfast
yesterday morning, all three of them. Heath and Betty and
their agent, I mean. Not the ginger fellow.
Mother said that at one point Heath excused himself to the
restroom, and he never came back. The other two got in a
fine panic over it, thinking he must have been sick or collapsed or something, but the restroom was empty."

Pearl made a mental note. "Which one's which, by the
way? Which one is Heath, I mean? I'm still a little unclear
on that."

Irene looked at her like she was a dunce. "The tall fellow,
Pearl. Gracious, didn't you read the paper?"

Violet Bourgo, bouncing her three-month-old on her hip,
said, "Then that rules out the two of them from the suspect
list, doesn't it? Charlie said they've been grilling poor Betty
Gardiner all morning, accusing her of having something to
do with it. Their theory is that she's jealous of him being
billed as the main star and so she set it all up. But Betty is so
torn up about it, I don't think she's involved."

"She could have hired someone to snatch him." Irene
sniffed. "No reason for her to dirty her own hands, but that
doesn't mean she's innocent. And she's an actress. She could
certainly act distraught if the situation called for it, whether
she felt it or not."

That much was true.

"You may have a point. Know what I heard?" Violet leaned over the bench they were sitting on, voice barely audible over the happy squeals and laughter of their children. "I heard one of those Hollywood producers wanted to turn Windy City Gumshoes *into a television show, but Heath Reynolds doesn't look right, so they were going to recast him. He was so angry he threatened to leave the show entirely, and Betty is furious with him."*

Pearl frowned. In her mind, Heath and Betty got along as famously as the brother and sister duo they played. They were a team. That was what Betty had said in an interview Pearl had read last month.

Though what did she expect? That the actress would admit there was tension between cast members to a reporter?

"Where did you hear that?" she asked Violet.

Violet gave a smug little smile. "Oh, you know. Around."

Pearl chuckled. "Not sure 'around' is really a credible source, Vi."

"My source is plenty credible. She overheard a conversation between the actors outside the hotel the other night." Violet sounded outraged at being questioned.

Irene snorted a laugh. "You mean your cousin Rose? She's as likely to make something up as repeat what she heard."

Pearl listened to the gossip for a while longer, but when Abigail got bored and then Ruth came over asking if they could walk to the soda shop, Pearl said goodbye to the other mothers.

Granted, it was still too early for a soda or an ice cream, but she wanted to walk around and listen to more talk. Maybe catch a glimpse of the "investigators" swarming the town, if she'd know them to see them.

Main Street was indeed full of unfamiliar people, and they weren't making any attempt to be discreet. The hats, magnifying glasses, the trench coats. One even had a pipe hooked in his mouth like he was Sherlock Holmes or something.

They looked exactly like a bunch of detectives would look in a movie. And as she pretended to run errands in a few different shops so she could get close enough to overhear them, her smile probably went as smug as Violet's. Because they sounded like a bunch of detectives from the movies too. Or, more particularly, like Joe from Windy City Gumshoes.

Their way of questioning, their intonation...sometimes their very words were lifted straight from her favorite episodes.

At eleven, she gave in and got two ice cream cones from the soda shop, sharing hers with a happy Abigail. Pearl was happy too.

Because she was pretty sure Suellen was right. Heath Reynolds wasn't missing at all. The cast of the show was just playing out a live-action drama for them, right here in town. Inviting them not only to solve the mystery of the coffee *princess before the episode in the series aired tomorrow night but to solve the mystery of Heath's disappearance as well.*

"Hey there, beautiful. You always smile so pretty at ice cream cones?"

Pearl spun at the familiar voice, giving an even bigger smile to Howard, who'd pulled up alongside her. "Sure do. Play your cards right, mister, and I'll share."

Howard put the car in park and hopped out, chuckling. "Well now, that's too tempting an offer to pass up. Want a ride home?"

"Daddy!" Ruth all but jumped into his arms, generously holding her cone to his lips. "Wanna bite?"

He obliged, making a few exaggerated "mm, mm" noises before shaking his head at a second offer. "Lunch first for me, Ruthie girl. Here, let's get you all in the car."

It required a bit of work, given the pram, but after a few minutes they were all situated inside, windows cracked to let in the pleasant air.

Peal turned to Howard as he pulled away from the curb. "I've figured it out."

He shot her a questioning look. "Figured what out? The coffee princess mystery? I thought we had our answer decided on for that. Don't change it on me now, honey. I've already got what I'm gonna say all figured out, when I call it in after lunch."

"No, no, not that. The Heath Reynolds disappearance thing. You've heard?"

Howard's face sobered. "It was all anyone was talking about at the factory. Sad, strange thing, isn't it? I hope he turns up."

"Oh, he will. In time for the big party tomorrow night, I'll bet." She leaned closer, pitching her voice low so it wouldn't risk seeping out the window. "It's a stunt, Howard. I'm sure of it."

She laid it all out for him on the ride home. The article that quoted "The Case of the Pharaoh's Curse," the investigators she'd overheard using Joe's lines all morning, the way they looked more like they were on a set than that they were really searching for a missing person.

She had a feeling that if she'd shared her theory with any of those women at the park, they would have scoffed at her. Howard, though, started out looking thoughtful, and by the time they pulled up at their house, he was downright excited.

"You know," he said as they carried the girls inside, "I bet you're right. And I bet that's part of the challenge. Think about it. Anyone, anywhere, in the country could solve the coffee princess mystery. The clues were right there, easy to piece together. They'll get thousands of people calling in. They can't have them all coming in for auditions though, can they?"

"I guess not. Though it would surely be limited by who could actually get to Kansas City next week."

"Exactly. They're trying to make this regional—probably a tip of the hat to their own roots, especially if Heath is related to the Reynolds who lived here. But even so, too many people could call in. Too many to audition. I bet that's why they're doing this. It's a publicity stunt, like you said. Get some extra attention, get people excited, sure. Imagine the fun when he shows up tomorrow night! But I bet it's also to see if anyone can figure it out. And that's how they'll actually decide who gets to audition. Because you'd have to be a longstanding fan of the show, wouldn't you? To pick up on all those lines they're using?"

Pearl pulled out a loaf of bread along with some meat and cheese. Her insides hummed, and she didn't think it was thanks to the sugar rush from the ice cream. "I bet you're right. So...how do we solve this one?"

Howard set four napkins on the counter. "Well, we already have some of the pieces, don't we? We know he's not really missing, but we know he's not at the hotel or with Mrs. Gardiner anymore either. So where would a fellow go to hide out around here for a few days? To avoid being seen?"

"The first step would be making everyone think that George Scott is Heath Reynolds, and vice versa."

Howard chuckled and doled bread out onto the napkins like they were cards. "Frank at the factory today had the same theory you do on that. He said the shorter one sounds like Heath, not the taller."

"If Frank and I are right, then it was Heath Reynolds in the cemetery yesterday." She peeled some ham slices off and set them on the bread. "His mother, most likely, is buried there."

"But in the Folmer plot. You want mustard or mayonnaise?" He spun for the icebox.

"Mayo for me. Ruth? What do you want on your sandwich, sweetie?"

"Cheese!" Ruth sat at the table, still in her sweater, kicking her feet in time to whatever song in her head had her bouncing on the seat.

Pearl stopped before adding ham to the third sandwich and reached for the cheese instead. "Cheese it is. You want any mayo? Or mustard?"

"Ew!"

Yesterday she'd wanted a piece of bread with only mayonnaise—but maybe that was what had made her decide it was "ew" today. "Just cheese then." She turned to Howard as he came back with the jar of mayo. "Suzanne Reynolds. In the Folmer plot, beside Bill Folmer's grave. Bill's widow is Lucy—I asked Mother when she called last night. She said she thought Lucy had a much younger brother somewhere."

"You're thinking that Heath is Lucy's brother?"

She shrugged. "The Folmer farm would be an easy place to hide, out away from town as it is."

Howard raised his eyebrows. "What do you say we take these sandwiches to go? Do a little sleuthing, Joe and Josie style?"

Pearl let out a breath. "You want to go snooping on someone else's property?"

"Snooping? Nah. We'll just drive by, see what we see. If we spot that car they've been going around town in, then maybe we pull in. If we're right, and this is part of the challenge, they'll be expecting some folks to put the pieces together and show up, won't they?"

"I guess so." She still didn't like the idea of barging in... but they wouldn't. Howard was right. They'd just see what they could see. Smiling, she folded the sandwiches into their napkins. "Okay. Let's do it. You wanna call your answer for the coffee princess case into the studio first?"

Howard plucked Abigail back out of the high chair he'd slid her into when they came in. "Later. Let's see if I can give them the answer to the second mystery along with the first."

Chapter Fifteen

*C*andlelight danced over the windows, music created a quiet undertone to the conversation, and Tracy swallowed the last bite of cheesecake with a satisfied sigh. "You know, I do believe this was better than what we could have gotten at a restaurant."

"Plus," Jeff added with a wiggle of his brows, "you get to wear your favorite shoes."

She glanced down at her fuzzy slippers and laughed. Until she got to her feet, she looked pretty great, if she did say so herself. She'd pulled a red dress out of her closet, curled her hair, and even put on evening makeup. Jeff had given her an appreciative whistle when he walked in an hour ago. Then he'd spotted the pink fuzzy slippers and laughed. "What can I say? No ensemble is complete without them."

"Or without this, perhaps?" He took a box from his pocket and slid it onto the table. It had the look of a jewelry box, though one of the larger ones.

"Jeff, I thought we said no presents! We're doing the gala, and I bought that new dress from Darla for it."

"Which is why you need that." He nudged the box a little closer. "Darla said so."

Tracy lifted her brows and reached for the box. "Really." Doubt saturated her tone.

The laughter in his eyes convinced her he meant it even before he spoke. "Really. She left me a voice mail at my office on Monday with instructions to call her back. When I did, she said she had my anniversary present for you all picked out, and all I had to do was swing by and get it. She said you needed it."

Tracy lifted the bow-bedecked lid of the box. She'd gone into Darling Darla's on Monday for her fitting, and Darla had basically acted like Tracy was a doll to be dressed up and adorned. She'd put headpieces, necklaces, bracelets, and what seemed like everything but the kitchen sink on her as Tracy stood there like a mannequin.

Including the long silver chain with pearls studded along it that now rested in this box, and the art-deco-style taper earrings. They'd been Tracy's favorites of the pieces, and she pulled out the long strand with a smile. It would be the perfect complement to the dress she'd pick up tomorrow. "I hope she gave you a good deal."

"I'm choosing to believe her when she said she did." Jeff put his elbows on the table. "I like her. I don't think we'll have a dull moment at the gala if we're sitting with her."

"Agreed." She'd made herself *not* talk about the contest while they ate. It was better to dream together about where they might travel this summer and reminisce about the thirty-two years they were celebrating. But now she told him about the call from Darla and the hint about the pharaoh's curse. She showed him the article that quoted the investigator who was looking for Heath and how his words were straight from the show.

Jeff sat back, eyes wide and sparkling. "Wow. So the whole disappearing act—it was just that. An act. It had to be. They had actors posing as investigators, using lines Heath Reynolds had written."

"And there's more. His name wasn't really Heath—it was Weiland. Or Way, as everyone called him after he moved here."

Jeff blinked a few times. "Okay. Spill it all."

She tugged him into the living room, where she'd set up the photographic evidence she and Robin had dug out of the attic, including the writings of "Chance McGee" that they suspected belonged to Way as well.

The set of Jeff's mouth said he was impressed. "I'm convinced. So that's half of the answer, anyway."

"Right." Tracy ran her tongue over her teeth as she surveyed the evidence before them. "It answers the question of what happened to 'Heath,' and in a way that only Canton could know. But it doesn't tell us what happened to his legacy. Why did he make the choice he did? Why did it lead to the end of his radio show? And why is Ronnie Paulsen so afraid of the story coming out? If *this* is all there is to it," she said, waving her hand, "he wouldn't be so scared that he'd come to town and try to sweet-talk me into publishing only something favorable."

"Wait—who's sweet-talking my wife?"

At his exaggerated huff, Tracy laughed. "Guess I didn't mention that part yet." She filled him in on the morning's visit, the stop at the cemetery where she found Way's grave, along with his family's, and the drive out to the Folmer farm. "I'm pretty sure we've been there before. Does it sound familiar to you?"

"Folmer." Jeff sank to a seat on the couch, eyes distant as he searched his memory. "Sort of. I think. But I couldn't tell you why. Think you can find the farm again?"

"Sure, it's not hard." She glanced at the window. "Well, in the daylight. No idea if I'd know where the turn was in the dark."

"I wasn't going to suggest we go now. But I don't have any classes in the morning. If you can spare the time, we could go for a little drive. Try to wrap this mystery up."

"That sounds perfect." She moved to sit beside him, but before she could, he stood again, wagging a finger at her.

"Nice try, Mrs. Doyle. No sitting and getting comfy yet. Those shoes are clearly made for dancing, and we'd better brush up before the big swing dance party this weekend, don't you think?"

There wasn't any big band music to be heard, but Tracy made no argument as Jeff swept her into his arms and led her around the living room. She just pressed her cheek to his shoulder and thanked the Lord that for all the unsolved mysteries in the world, this wasn't one of them. She never had to wonder whether her husband loved her. And that made the night shine.

Frost coated the world in a spectacular design of crystal patterns as beautiful as snow the next morning. Tracy stepped outside with wonder, her gaze tracking over each etching on glass and metal. "Wow."

Jeff was a couple steps behind her, but his reaction echoed hers. "Wow. I don't remember the last time we had a frost like this."

She'd thought at first, when she glanced out the window, that snow had fallen overnight, which would have thrown a wrench in their plans if the plows hadn't made it out yet. But no, the roads were all clear. Only grass and rooftops and cars had been painted with the magic of the frost, thick and beautiful. "Me neither. Look at the designs on the glass. Almost like feathers."

Jeff lifted his cell phone and snapped a picture. "There. Now I won't have to wonder next time when the last time was."

She chuckled and followed him to the car, taking a sip of her coffee from her travel mug as Jeff started the engine.

It felt weird, climbing into one car together on a weekday morning. Usually, even if Jeff didn't have an early class, he spent the time at the college, grading papers, preparing his next lecture, or meeting with students or other professors. It made the day feel like a holiday.

They passed Amy and the kids on their way to school, and at the confused look her sister sent her, Tracy stuck her tongue out and wiggled her fingers in the same mocking gesture they'd been using since they were kids. Then she pulled out her phone to send her a text. SOLVING MYSTERIES. ROBIN AND I FOUND LOTS OF INFO YESTERDAY. CALL WHEN YOU GET HOME, IF YOU HAVE TIME, AND I'LL UPDATE YOU.

"What's that look for?" Jeff asked when she just sat there for a minute, holding the phone in her hands without sending the message.

She shook herself out of her funk and hit the button. "Nothing."

"Tracy."

Bother. He knew her too well. She heaved a sigh. "It's really nothing. Or *should* be nothing. No, it really is nothing. I just keep having all these 'will she even have time to talk to me?' thoughts, which are utterly ridiculous. It's not like I didn't have time to talk to her after I got married and had kids."

Jeff reached over and took her hand. "True. And I'm sure Amy will make sure she has time for you too. But she did just double the size of her family, and obviously they all have a lot of adjusting to do. I think it's actually very considerate of you to have that in mind when you're asking for her time."

"Aw." She gave his fingers a squeeze. "I love you, you know that? You always take my hang-ups and turn them into something that sounds like a virtue."

He laughed and asked her which way to turn at the next corner.

Soon they were heading out of town on the same county road she'd taken yesterday. The farther they drove, the more Jeff's face got that cute little wrinkle between his brows that said he was thinking.

"It's right up ahead," she said when they rounded the final turn before the farm. "On the left."

He slowed and got a good look at the place. "Tracy," he said in a musing tone as he continued past, "you weren't wrong. We've been here."

"I knew it. What was it for? A wedding or something? I have this image of a party."

"Party, yes. Wedding, no." He pulled into the same driveway she had yesterday to turn around and backtrack, giving her a strange look. "That's Julie's house."

"Julie." She blinked at him once, her brain not making the connection between the Folmer farm and the name Julie. Then it clicked. "Julie Missenden?"

"Married name, of course. But they live here on her family's property. Don't you remember? We came to a faculty party she and Tyler hosted a few years ago—probably ten years or so."

That explained the snippets of memory about a party, then. And also the feel of it she'd maintained. All adults, the talk more elevated than other gatherings she'd attended. Because the party guests were college professors. "I remember now. That's when I got to listen in on that fascinating theology debate. Julie was a great hostess."

"Uh huh." Now he sounded amused.

No doubt because Tracy was lost in piecing together the memories of that evening instead of asking the obvious question. "Right. So…what does this mean? That Julie Missenden is related to Heath Reynolds? Or Way, or whatever we're calling him?"

"I think so. I don't actually know her family history, aside from the fact that her dad ran this place as a farm, but when she inherited, she didn't attempt to keep the agriculture part running. Didn't have to, of course. Tyler's doing pretty well for himself with his software company."

"Well enough that they could sponsor this contest, do you think?" She tapped a finger against the lid of her cup. "Because obviously Julie isn't *entering* the contest, if this is her family. She already knows who Heath really was, she has to. He'd have been…what, her uncle? He couldn't have been her father. The obituary said he had no kids."

"Uncle or great-uncle, maybe. And yeah. He's doing that well, I'm pretty sure. Julie's mentioned a few things over the years, just in passing."

"Wow. Okay."

"Wishing you'd gone into computer software instead of journalism?" Jeff asked, a tease in his tone.

She wrinkled her nose. "No way. Wishing *you* had."

He laughed and wove their fingers together again. "Right. So… what now? Go see if Julie's in her office this morning?"

Was it sporting to corner her on campus? The thought made her bite back a sigh. "Well, phooey. Mary Jane Shoemaker already made this connection, I think. A week ago. When I was distracted by threats of libel."

"But you rescued Julie, right? Maybe she didn't tell her anything."

"Maybe." In which case, she probably wouldn't tell *them* anything either. But that was okay. Tracy was an old hand at learning from what people didn't say.

Chapter Sixteen

*T*racy had been to Culver-Stockton College many times over the years, of course, but she mostly just knew her way to Jeff's office and a few of the buildings where they hosted events she'd attended. As she followed him through the corridors, her eyes moving over all the numbers and names on the doorplates, she had to smile to see how at home he was here. This was his place, his element. She'd seen him in it countless times, but it never got old, really. She loved hearing students and faculty alike calling out greetings to him with obvious respect.

He led her past his own office into an adjoining hallway and straight to one of the last two doors. He knocked, and Tracy recognized Julie's voice telling them to come in even before she saw the nameplate on the wall beside the door. Dr. Julie Missenden.

Jeff opened the door with a smile and ushered Tracy in ahead of him. "Morning, Julie," he said. "This a bad time?"

Julie had a stack of papers in front of her and a pen in hand, but she smiled and tossed the pen to the desk without the least hesitation. "Are you kidding? A break sounds awesome. Some of these things are just painful."

Jeff laughed and took a seat in front of her desk. "Don't I know it. But then there are the ones that make you see something in a whole new way. Those make it all worthwhile."

179

"Don't they?" Julie leaned back in her chair, stretching her arms. She wore a gorgeous sweater in turquoise with a silver thread winking through it. "You two here about the contest?"

Jeff grinned. "Yep. We're not the first to make the connection between you and Heath—or rather, Weiland—are we?"

"To make the connection to me being a Folmer and Way being my uncle? No." She smiled. "But that was the easy part. There are plenty of folks around who remember my maiden name. And Uncle Way."

Tracy nodded. "I was kinda surprised to realize *I* do. He and my grandpa were friends."

"I remember," Julie said. "Uncle Way always called him one of his first friends in town. I guess it was the bowling thing. He was a fair bit older than your grandfather, wasn't he?"

Tracy nodded again. "About ten years, I think."

"Funny how much that matters when we're young, and how little once we're all adults, isn't it?" Julie chuckled, her gaze going distant for a second before snapping back to them. "I figured I'd be seeing you soon after I spotted you in the cemetery yesterday, Tracy."

"I was only there because I was following someone else."

Julie's brows rose, a smile playing at the corners of her mouth. "Who? Darla? Mary Jane?"

If only. Tracy shook her head. "Ronnie Paulsen."

The shift was quick and complete. Pleasant expression gone, replaced by a cold shudder that slammed down over her features. Not one meant to keep them out, she didn't think. Just the kind meant to keep her emotions *in*. "Oh. *Him*. He dropped by the newspaper, I take it? Tried to threaten you into keeping everything hush-hush?"

"Pretty much." Not that yesterday's visit had been threatening, per se, but the email certainly had been. "I followed him when he left. He went to the cemetery, which I found pretty strange. And then out to your farm?" That last part she delivered as a fact but aimed like a question.

"I know. Tyler was working from home, so he got to deal with him this time."

"This time?" Jeff leaned forward, elbows braced on the wooden arms of the chair.

Now when Julie looked from one of them to the other, it seemed like she was debating how much to say. After a moment, she tossed her hands up. "Not like I can actually give you the answers—that was the whole point to this contest. I know what brought my uncle here, and I know why he stayed. But I have no idea why I meet a brick wall every time I try to dig into his history. What happened that Ronnie Paulsen doesn't want anyone to know about?"

"That's the real question then. The real mystery we're trying to solve." Jeff quirked a brow. "And no one else has solved it yet?"

Julie shook her head. "There have been some answers turned in, but they're not complete. They've just said that his legacy faded away when he moved here to care for his sister. There's more to it than that though. There has to be." She sighed. "All I wanted was an encouraging story to tell my grandson. Yet when I asked a few questions, I had radio bigwigs threatening me with lawsuits. And I have no idea why."

Tracy scoured her mind, trying to remember any recent mentions of Julie's grandchildren. They'd been praying for one of them a couple years ago. The request had come through the college system. It had been pretty serious… Diabetes, that was it. He'd been diagnosed with Type 1 at the age of twelve. "Carson? He's the one you wanted to tell this story to?"

Julie's face softened. "He's been such a champ since the diagnosis. We were so afraid when he was in the hospital. He could have died, if his mom hadn't taken him in right away. We all thought it was just the flu. It hasn't been easy for him, learning a whole new way of life. He's doing great, overall, but he's also struggling at the thought of giving up his dreams. He's wanted to follow in his father's footsteps ever since he was really little. To join the Air Force and be a pilot. But that's one of the few things still forbidden to diabetics."

It wasn't something Tracy had ever had to learn about for her own family, but Amy had taught several kids with Type 1 diabetes in her classes over the years, so she'd heard some stories about the scares from sudden low blood sugars—kids passing out on the playground—or lashing out in anger when their numbers were too high. The science around the disease had come a long way in recent years, but still. It was scary, and it had to be hard on Carson when it threatened his dreams. "That must be rough."

Julie's smile was sad. "He'll find another dream. I know he will. But that's why I wanted to tell him about Uncle Way. Heath Reynolds, the radio star, who gave it all up. He walked away at the height of his career to take care of his sister—my grandmother." She sighed. "That's what killed her, you know. Diabetes. She was diagnosed as an adult, after she'd had her kids, which was pretty unusual, I think. They still called it juvenile diabetes back then. But it was such early days for treatment. Insulin had only been in use for a decade or so, and testing blood sugar practically required a lab. By the time she was fifty, it was killing her. Organ damage, foot issues, eyesight failing. After my grandfather died, she couldn't do it on her own. She didn't tell anyone, of course, stubborn farm wife that she was. My dad said they had no idea, not until she collapsed one day and they called him from the hospital."

"Oh, man." It had all happened well before her time—before her parents' time, even—but Tracy still felt emotional hearing the story. "I'm so sorry."

"I never met her, of course, but Dad told so many stories, and so did Uncle Way. That's why he moved here. To take care of her in her final years." Julie straightened again and lifted her chin. "Only, he didn't let it steal his dreams. That's what I want Carson to see. It just redirected them. He found new ways to be the man God had made him. Carson may have inherited some unwanted genetics when it comes to diabetes, but he inherited *that* too. The grit and determination. The passion. Reynolds blood means a whole lot more than some wacky sugars."

Grit and determination laced Julie's voice too and made Tracy smile. Here was a grandmother fighting for her grandson in some pretty creative ways. And Tracy would do anything she could to help with that. "I hope Carson is inspired by your family's story. He's, what, fourteen now?"

"Just turned fifteen. Been growing like a weed." Julie ran a finger under each eye. "He's going to do great things. I know he is."

"I don't doubt it for a second," Tracy said.

"And we're going to bust down a few of those brick walls for you. Aren't we, honey?" Jeff held out a hand to her.

"You bet we are." She squeezed his fingers and then let him haul her to her feet. "That Paulsen guy doesn't know who he's messing with. The more he tries to block the truth, the more determined we all are to find it." She chuckled. "I mean, if *I* can't, I'll just sic Mary Jane Shoemaker on him."

Julie laughed. "Don't think I haven't considered that. Between you guys and her and Darla Franklin, I don't think this mystery stands a chance."

"Uh oh," Jeff said as he opened the car door for Tracy a few moments later. "I know that look. What are you planning?"

"I don't know that I'm *planning* anything, exactly. Just…considering a new method of attack." She met his gaze, easing onto the seat without swinging her legs inside, which meant he stood there, leaning on the open door. "How determined are you to win those cruise tickets?"

Jeff quirked a brow.

Tracy smiled. "Julie got me thinking. Mary Jane, Darla, us and Robin…we all bring something different to the table. On our own, any one of us is pretty formidable when it comes to rooting out information."

Jeff's puzzled expression turned into a smile. "You're thinking maybe we all need to join forces."

An idea that had probably been stirring since Darla dropped that clue in her lap yesterday. Why else would she have done it but for a sense of camaraderie and a desire for Tracy to have the satisfaction of an answer? Even if Darla had already turned in her answer and wanted to win, she wanted something else more. Something Tracy wanted too.

Answers for Julie's sake. And the joy of working with new friends and beloved family. "I know the Missendens aren't going to spring for *six* tickets—that's insane. But honestly, who cares about the prize? I just want to figure this out, and I'll sign over any claim to the prize if it'll get those two forces of nature on board."

Jeff nodded. "I'm game. I'd feel a little weird claiming the prize anyway, now that I know it's sponsored by my friend and colleague. But do you think you can convince them of that?"

"I have no idea. But there's only one way to find out."

While Jeff drove her back to the house, she called Robin. Then she called the women who had, at least in her estimation, proven themselves the stiffest competition. She asked if they'd meet her and Robin at Buttermilk Bakeshop in an hour. Darla agreed without hesitation, of course, with not so much as a hint of suspicion in her tone.

Mary Jane was a bit more wary, but, ultimately, she agreed. "Since you did such a nice write-up about Pat's grandparents," she finally said. "Sure."

Jeff came into the house with her long enough to grab his briefcase then planted a kiss on her lips. "For fortification," he said when he pulled away, winking. "You're going to need it. If you guys need backup, give me a call. I can bring the football team with me."

She snorted a laugh. "I don't know, honey. I think my ladies could take a few football players. Now, if you had a rugby team…"

He strode to the door, chuckling along with her. "Call me after the meeting. I want to know how it goes."

"Will do."

In the time remaining before she was due at the bakery, she sent Annette a quick update via email, promising to be in after lunch and then asking if anyone had dug anything up on Ronnie Paulsen and WRMC Chicago.

Because if she knew anything about her colleagues, it was that they could all do a fair imitation of a dog with a bone when it came to potential stories.

Her phone rang, and Annette's name popped up about two beats after she hit send on the email. "Funny you should ask," Annette said in response to Tracy's hello. "I don't think Eric's done much else since that man had the nerve to come into the office yesterday."

Tracy reached for a notepad and pen. "And?"

"And, perhaps not surprisingly, WRMC Chicago is in what one might call pretty dire straits."

It really wasn't all that surprising. Tracy had written more than one article over the years about radio stations folding or consolidating and about ad sponsors being harder and harder to come by. In addition to the competition from television, traditional stations were competing with satellite radio and, even worse, with phone apps. "I'm shocked."

"I know, right? I think Eric wanted me to be impressed that he found evidence of that, but I'd assumed as much. Not that assumptions should inform a story, of course."

Tracy thought for a moment. "If WRMC is in a precarious position, that could be why Ronnie Paulsen is desperate to keep any bad press away. One article that paints them in a bad light—even from something that happened seventy-five years ago—could get picked up by a Chicago paper and convince one or more sponsors to back out of an ad spot they need."

"Not a fun place to be in. We can all relate to that here."

"Too true." Thanks to Eric's vision and everyone's hard work, the *Lewis County Times* had passed out of the danger zone for now.

But newspapers still folded just as fast as radio stations, and none of them were comfortable enough to think they could get lazy. "But the answer isn't to threaten. Hence, I suppose, the attempt yesterday to smooth things over."

"Guess so."

Knowing that the radio station was struggling didn't tell her what that bad press was, but at least it solidified the motivation for all the brick walls. "Something must have happened between Heath Reynolds and Alfie Paulsen. Ronnie called it a debacle that nearly put Alfie out of business," Tracy said. "But how can we figure out what?"

Maybe one of her new potential allies would have an idea. And maybe they'd share it.

A "maybe" that seemed more fantasy than possibility when she met up with Robin on the sidewalk twenty minutes later. They entered the bakery on a gust of cold wind and saw that both Darla and Mary Jane had beaten them there—and each had chosen a table on opposite sides of the seating area.

Granted, in the small café, that didn't actually put much space between them, but it still seemed to represent the dilemma. How was she to convince them to work together—and with her and Robin?

A question that demanded more coffee. They stood in line for their cups, Tracy waving to the ladies when they each spotted her. Ordinarily she would have splurged on a pastry too, but she *might* have had a slice of cheesecake for breakfast already.

Coffee in hand, she led Robin first to Darla, who was closest. "Morning. Would you please come over here with us?"

Darla lifted her brows but dutifully picked up her own coffee and éclair and followed them to the opposite side of the shop. She didn't even object when Tracy indicated she should take the open seat at Mary Jane's table. Tracy grabbed a spare chair from against the wall and pulled it up to the little three-top.

Mary Jane's white brows were knit. "Okay, you have my attention. Hi, Darla."

Darla smiled. "Morning, MJ. Have you heard from the kids yet?"

Mary Jane shook her head. "Not since that text saying they'd landed safe and sound. You?"

Darla mirrored the headshake. "Though I expect them to start flooding my phone with a bunch of photos soon enough."

Tracy's confusion must have shone on her face, because Darla chuckled and reached over to pat her hand. "Sorry, dear. Guess you had no reason to make that connection. My second daughter is married to Mary Jane's oldest son. Their kids took them to the Caribbean for a ten-day stay, the lucky bums."

They were related? Or in-laws, anyway? Tracy gusted out a breath and exchanged a glance with Robin. "Okay." She wasn't sure what that meant. Did these women who had seemed like such rivals in fact eat holiday meals together? Were they friends, or the sort of in-laws that never talked to each other? "That sounds lovely."

Mary Jane sighed. "Doesn't it? I can't remember the last time Pat and I got away for more than a weekend."

"Because Pat won't take more than a day off. Yet you think you'll be able to convince him to go on that river cruise?" Darla shook her head again. "He'll never go for it. You might as well—"

"I am *not* giving up on the contest, Darla." Mary Jane punctuated her statement with a swig of whatever drink she had in her cup. "It's my one shot at something more than a camping trip."

"Oh boy," Robin muttered, too low for the older ladies to hear.

Tracy grunted a quiet agreement. This was not the argument she'd hoped to find herself in the middle of. She looked up and waved a hello when Lincoln Bailey strode into the shop. He flashed her a smile and waved back, not detouring from his beeline for the counter.

Just as well.

"I'm only pointing out what would be obvious had you bothered looking at your husband's face when Ken announced the contest." Darla leaned toward Tracy, her eyes twinkling. "A bunch of us have a weekly get-together, you know. Finger foods and the radio programs. *Jukebox Saturday Night* and then *Turn Back the Dial*. It's us and the Shoemakers and the Kramers and the Clarks. Been doing it for over a decade now, every week. Well, more or less."

The Franklins, the Shoemakers, the Kramers, and the Clarks. Names she'd come to know well as they'd come in, one by one, looking for archived newspapers—and all very concerned that the others had beaten them to the punch. "Wait a minute. So you all hang out every week? And you heard about the contest at the same time—"

"And the race was on!" Darla said with a laugh, brandishing a finger in the air like it was a starter's pistol. She even added a little bugle call.

Mary Jane rolled her eyes, but she was smiling. Mary Jane Shoemaker—*smiling*. "I don't know why the others are bothering. I'm going to win this thing."

"Some of us are taking it a bit too seriously," Darla said in a stage whisper to Tracy. Then she smiled too. "But not me. I say the more competition the merrier. The joy is in the chase, right?"

Tracy lifted her brows. "Is that why you gave me a hint yesterday?"

"She—you *what?*" Mary Jane sent Darla an exasperated look. "You're a crazy person. If you're so determined to have more people in on the drawing for the prize, why not just announce the answer in the paper?"

Darla didn't look perturbed. "Tracy's been so sweet. I couldn't bear the thought of her not figuring it out."

For a second, Tracy felt a bolt of defensiveness, that Darla thought she *needed* the help. But then amusement crept in. After all, both women had been well ahead of her in many ways so far. "About that answer. I was talking to Julie, and she said that a couple people had turned in answers already that were partly right, but no one had figured out why the legacy of Heath Reynolds and *Windy City Gumshoes* was so thoroughly buried."

"It's more than just his moving here? Phooey." Darla scowled. "And we can only turn in one answer!"

"Guess that means you're out of the running." Mary Jane looked downright smug.

Tracy took another sip of her coffee. "You have me curious, Darla. I'm assuming you'd already called in your answer when you gave me that tip yesterday. How did you figure it out so quickly?"

Darla looked like she'd keep smiling until the end of time. "My dad was the chief of police when the cast came to Canton. I remembered him saying how it was all a publicity stunt and that Way—Heath Reynolds—had come to him as soon as he got to town and told him the plan. He wanted him to know that nothing bad was actually happening, so there was no reason to be alarmed or to get irritated by the supposed investigators that showed up. It was one of his favorite stories, especially after he retired." Her smile faded. "Guess it wasn't enough though. Dad certainly never told any tales about why the show vanished from awareness. I assumed that was just the natural course of things, when it went off the air and television took over more and more."

Tracy sighed. "A reasonable assumption, if the heir to the record company—or its radio station parent company, anyway—hadn't started threatening Julie and the paper for digging into the story."

"What?" Mary Jane came to attention, eyes wide. "That just reeks of having something to hide, doesn't it?"

Tracy nodded. "It does. But honestly, I don't know how we're going to get to the bottom of it in the day we have left—not alone." Her smile passed the baton to Robin.

"That's why we thought we'd enlist your help," Robin said. "Maybe if we all put together the pieces we've gathered, we'll see something that'll lead to the full answer."

Mary Jane blinked at her. "You can't really expect us to all band together so that *you* can claim the prize?"

Robin laughed. "I was never in it to begin with. My husband gets horrible seasickness. I'm helping Tracy for the fun of the mystery."

Tracy spread her hands on the table. "And Jeff and I are out of the running. We agreed that the prize doesn't matter to us at this point. We just want to help Julie find the answers." When Mary Jane looked dubious, Tracy very nearly rolled her eyes. "You want me to sign a legal document promising that? Hey, Lincoln!"

She only hailed him because Lincoln walked by at that very moment, and it was simply too convenient to pass up.

He smiled and moved to stand near their table. "Morning, ladies. Or…" He paused, checked his watch, and nodded. "Yep, still morning. How are you all doing today?"

"Not bad." Tracy smiled. "And I'm happy to see this cold snap will be ending tomorrow. Robin and I weren't looking forward to braving the cold in our lovely gala dresses on Saturday if it was still going to be so cold."

"Ah, you all will be at the Swingin' Gala? Excellent. Melody and I have tickets too."

"Oh, good!" Robin said. "We'll see you there."

Tracy nodded. "In the meantime, I have a question for you."

Mary Jane folded her arms over her stomach, muttering, "All right, all right. I believe you."

Good. Though seeing Lincoln sent her mind on an entirely different path than it had traveled thus far. "Say, Lincoln...what do you know about show-biz contracts? Between, say, a writer and voice actor and the company that produced his show?"

"Well, it's not my area of expertise, per se, but I've read a few." Lincoln pulled a chair out from the neighboring table and sat down with a smile. A sure sign that he had some helpful information to impart. "There's a lot of variation within them, of course, but generally speaking, whatever was drawn up between the creator and the producer would grant certain rights to each of them, along with royalties—payment based on performance—and a percentage of profits from direct sales, ad revenue generated, and so on. Usually, the producer or publisher controls granting someone else the right to produce the story in another format, like books or television."

Tracy tapped the lid of her coffee cup. Would Way Reynolds have been in breach of contract if he'd moved here instead of finishing out the series? But how would that have reflected poorly on SongBird Records?

Chapter Seventeen

The Folmer farm, like all the other farms around, lay dormant and brown, stretching out in colorless fields toward the river. In another month or two, the tractors would rumble to life, the grass would start growing, and spring planting would become the race that ruled the area. For now, though, the farms all lay sleepy and sad-looking, little by way of color to liven them up.

The blue Cadillac gleamed bright and bold in the sunshine, a beacon that caught Pearl's eye the moment they came around the turn in the road. Howard laughed and slapped the steering wheel when he spotted it. "Well, look at that! We were right, dollface." He said it in the same intonation Joe and Josie's landlord always used when talking to Josie, who didn't much like being called dollface.

Pearl grinned. "I knew it. Though...are you sure we ought to go down there?"

Howard already had his turn signal on. "Why not? Looks like quite a collection of cars there already, and I can't imagine they all belong to the Folmers."

The "collection" included an old farm truck, the blue Cadillac the radio folks had been driving around, and a Ford that looked like the ones half the town owned, themselves included.

What convinced her not to argue, however, was the sign that came into view as Howard drove their car slowly down the lane. It was nothing fancy, just a scrap piece of wood painted white with black letters proclaiming, WINDY CITY GUMSHOES FANS! GET YOUR SCRIPTS HERE!

"Hot dog." Howard drummed the wheel again. "Look at that, honey."

"I'm looking," she said with a laugh then glanced into the back seat. Abigail had dozed off—no surprise, given how close it was to nap time—and Ruth had finished her sandwich and looked rather drowsy herself.

Howard pulled in behind the other Ford, and Pearl glanced around for some indication of where they ought to go. Maybe there would be a sign directing guests to a particular door or something. She hoped so.

"Want to come with us, sweetie, or stay here for a minute?" Howard asked Ruth.

Her answer was a yawn, her eyes drifting closed. "Stay."

Howard looked at Pearl. She shrugged. In town she wouldn't leave the kids in the car unattended for more than a minute, but out here? The windows of the car were all down a little to let in the unusually warm breeze, and Pearl would stay on the porch to keep an eye and an ear on them. She'd certainly left the baby napping in their own driveway before when it was nice out, since Abigail never went back to sleep if they tried to transfer her to her crib.

Once she was out of the car, Pearl saw that a woman sat on a rocker on the porch. She seemed familiar, though Pearl probably wouldn't have had the name to go with the face were it not in context. "Hello, Mrs. Folmer," she called.

Lucy Folmer turned her face their way and smiled, but her eyes searched and settled in a way that left Pearl wondering if she could see them. "Afternoon. Forgive me. My eyesight isn't what it used to be, and I don't recognize your voice. You are...?"

"Howard and Pearl Allen, ma'am," Howard said.

Lucy Folmer's face wrinkled momentarily in thought then smoothed again. "Oh! Were you a Wallace, Pearl?"

"That's right. Vivian and Nicholas's oldest daughter." She took Howard's arm as he led her toward the porch.

"Are you here about my brother's contest?" Her smile lit up her face. "So clever, isn't he? Cleverest writer I've ever seen. He's going places, that Weiland. I've been telling him so all his life."

"At the moment, Lu, the only place I want to go is right here." The screen door squeaked open, and a man stepped out. The shorter, square-jawed man who'd given Pearl the lollipop on Monday. He wore a cardigan instead of a trench coat, and a broad smile that he aimed at Pearl and Howard. "Hello there, friends. Where's the little lady today?"

He actually remembered her? Pearl motioned to the car. "Sleeping, I hope. Though if she suspected the 'lollipop man' was here, as she's taken to calling you, she'd be awake and out of the car in a heartbeat."

Mr. Reynolds—because obviously she'd been right to deduce that was who he was—chuckled and held out a hand toward Howard. "Way Reynolds. Please call me Way. Or Heath, if you're like my agent and don't care for my given name."

"Howard Allen." Howard shook, looking like he might just burst from the pleasure of it all. "Honor to meet you, Way. My wife and I are big fans of your work."

Way waved that off. "Aw, thanks, but it wouldn't be much without the rest of the crew. The editors—and Betty! She really brings it to life, doesn't she? Great gal. I've said for years she's the heart of the show. They could replace me a dozen times over and no one would notice, as long as she stays."

Something about the way he said it made Pearl frown. "You're not leaving, are you?"

Way flashed them a smile, his voice bright, but darted a sheepish look at his sister. "Not forever, I hope. But I'm pretty desperate for a sabbatical. I've been trying to convince my sister to let me rest and recuperate here for a little while."

Mrs. Folmer's eyes might not have seen so well anymore, but her hearing was clearly spot-on. She rolled her eyes. "You're not fooling anyone, Weiland. You don't need a break. You think you need to take care of me. And like I told you a month ago, I won't have it. You're not going to give up your career for me, when you've finally made your big break."

"Who said anything about giving it up? Just a little holiday, that's all. A month or two. I've already got it written into the script. Oh! Speaking of which." He beamed a smile at Pearl and Howard again. "You two are the first to show up. Have the answers for me?"

Howard, looking pleased as a peacock, nodded. "Sure do. The first part, about the coffee princess—that was easy. I mean, the easier bit than knowing to show up here," he added quickly, when amused offense flickered over Way's face. "She planned to run off and marry the plantation owner, but her father got wind of it. He hired the goons to kidnap her when he couldn't talk her out of it. Only she gave them the slip in Peoria. That's when he hired Joe and Josie, never thinking they'd pick up on the fact he'd had something to do with it."

Way nodded along, smiling at the end. "Right on all counts, Mr. Allen."

"Call me Howard." He grinned. "Now, as for the last piece of the puzzle and whether that was her body that turned up in Kansas City—no way. She faked her death to put the goons and her father off the scent, and if you ask me, Josie's going to figure it out and help her get away, down to Colombia and her true love."

"Josie, huh? Not Joe?" Way sat on the arm of the rocking chair beside his sister's.

Howard shook his head. "Joe's too distracted by that other—say!" His eyes went wide, and he slapped a hand to his forehead. "That's how you're going to write him out for a while! He's distracted by that note he just got from his war buddy. Josie's going to have to finish this up on her own, and he's going to go off investigating what happened to Max."

Way nodded. "And Alfie tried to tell me it wouldn't work. He said it was illogical."

"I think it makes fine sense. We can get caught up with Joe when he comes back, and Josie can be trying to hold the fort down by herself in Chicago. Some fun conflict there, I'd think."

Pearl had to put in her two cents. "Josie's a swell PI, but she doesn't like working alone. She's going to need some sort of partner, even if it's only for a few months."

"Ah." Holding up a finger, Way stepped back inside for a second. He must have grabbed something from just inside the doorway. Papers, she saw a moment later. Bound at the corner with a metal brad. "The lady has a very good point." He held the stack of papers out toward them.

Howard reached to take it. "The script for the next episode," he said, tapping the episode number. "'The Case of the Other Joe.'"

Pearl leaned in close when Howard flipped to the first page. "Oh, how fun! This is her interim partner? Is he really named Joe too?"

Way chuckled. "Thought it would be a fun twist. Potential love interest for her too, though we'll have to see how the fans respond to the first few episodes."

Sure sounded interesting to Pearl.

"Is that another car coming, Way?" Mrs. Folmer said from her chair. She was rocking, though Pearl only just then noticed that she wasn't wearing shoes. Her feet were wrapped in bandages.

She didn't know why, or how long her recovery would take, but it was no wonder Mr. Reynolds wanted to take a few months to care for her. How would a farmer's widow manage around here, if she could neither walk nor see clearly? Even if they weren't plowing and planting this year, Pearl heard the clucking of chickens and the rooting of pigs that promised unending work to do.

Mr. Reynolds squinted toward the lane and sighed. "Yeah. But not competition for you in the audition, Howard. It's just Alfie."

Alfie must be Alfie Paulsen, the producer that Betty Gardiner had mentioned in that interview. Pearl looked toward the lane too, her eyes going a little wider at the flashy red roadster that barreled along at a speed that sent up a dust cloud behind it. Shouldn't Alfie be taking a little more care with what must be a pricey car?

A moment later the roadster came to a screeching halt, throwing up dust and gravel. Dust and gravel that pelted their Ford and no doubt billowed into their open windows.

"Hey!" Ordinarily, Pearl wouldn't have said anything about noise and dust. But her babies were in that car. She hurried down the porch steps, wincing when the slam of the car door was followed by a startled wail from the back seat.

The redhaired man she'd seen on Monday barely spared her a glance as he sped by, waving papers in his hand and yelling, "I told you, Reynolds! Breach of contract!"

Pearl opened the car door and reached for Abigail, whose first surprised cry had stretched into more. Ruth was still asleep, curled up on the seat. "Shh. I've got you, baby," Pearl said as she held Abigail against her, bouncing and swaying to try to get her to settle back down.

The crying at least gave way to whimpers, and Abigail hooked her thumb in her mouth, but her eyes didn't slide closed again. Not yet anyway.

Pearl swayed with her toward the porch. She'd missed whatever response Way had made to his producer, but *whatever it was must not have appeased the man. He shook his head furiously.*

"I don't care. That's not what the contract said—what you signed, what you agreed to."

"Nowhere in there does it say I can't miss a few weeks!" Way folded his arms over his chest, looking more than a little irritated. "Good heavens, man, don't I deserve a vacation? I've been writing an episode a week for five years!"

"We've tried to bring in other writers to help you out. It's not my fault none of them got the 'tone' right and that you're so picky about the final product."

"Which I'm allowed to be, per that contract you're waving around," Way said. "And I never vetoed those writers entirely, I just said they needed more practice. You're the one who gave them one shot and then sent them packing."

"Because the competition is too fierce in this business to let quality slip for even one episode. Yet here you are talking about a months-long leave, when we're teetering on the brink."

Mrs. Folmer stretched out a hand toward her brother, her face concerned. "Weiland? Is that true? Will the show fail if you take this time off?"

"No, Lu," he said, shooting visual daggers at his colleague. He took his sister's hand in his, folding his other over her fingers. "We're doing just fine. Don't you worry about that."

"Fine?" Alfie barked out a laugh. "You can lie to your sister all you want, Heath, but we both know it's all going to come crashing down if you step away."

"He's exaggerating," Way said to Lucy. He turned back to Alfie. "Especially because I'll still be writing. I told you that—I'll write the episodes here and send them straight up to Chicago each week. Got it all lined up. And the storyline supports it. Isn't that right, Howard?"

Howard had apparently skimmed a bit more of the script while the men argued, given the page he was on. He nodded enthusiastically. "I think it's a swell twist. Real good."

Alfie snorted. "Sure, let's take the word of a Missouri bumpkin."

"Hey!" Pearl said again. She had a few visual daggers of her own to throw his way. "Didn't your mother teach you any manners?"

"My mother taught me the value of a buck, dollface, and the power of a contract."

Pearl's hackles rose at that dollface, delivered just like the landlord did in the show—only from Paulsen, it sounded natural. Probably where Way had borrowed it from. She had a feeling Betty Gardiner shared Pearl's reaction in life then translated it onto the air.

Alfie turned back to Reynolds. "And what happens when Betty wants to go out on maternity leave, huh? You think *that's not coming any day now? What'll the show do without Joe or Josie?"*

"She's already said she plans to work around having kids—"

"Oh sure, that's what they all say. And maybe she'd pull it off for a while, on the radio show. At least for that it won't matter when she looks like that." He waved a dismissive, disgusted hand toward Pearl and her rounded belly.

She had to step in front of Howard to keep him from charging forward. No matter what Alfie thought of the maternal form, it was no reason to pick a fight.

Though she hoped and prayed he didn't have a wife at home he insulted like that.

Paulsen didn't even seem to notice their reaction. "Know what I think? I think you're deliberately sabotaging the radio show so you can focus on that television deal."

Way shook his head. "I told you I have no interest in that. I'm not a film actor, Alfie. I don't want that notoriety. I don't want people recognizing me everywhere I go. We couldn't have George pretending to be me anymore for public appearances if everyone knew what I look like."

"I don't know why you do that," Mrs. Folmer muttered. "You're a good-looking man, Weiland. Just like Dad. You'd make a fine TV star, I say."

"You're biased." He gave her hand another pat. "And it doesn't matter whether I can compare to Cary Grant or not—I still don't want that kind of attention. Makes me uncomfortable. Which," he said, looking at Alfie again, "I've told you time and again. That's why I retained the television rights. Not so I could sell them and cut you out of the deal and write for the screen instead of the airwaves."

Alfie shook his head and jabbed a finger at Way. "You love your ideas. You love your stories, your characters. You don't care a whit about the means for getting them out there. I've heard you say it yourself. Books, radio, television—doesn't matter to you. Well, let me tell you something, buster. It matters to me. I have a lot people I'm responsible for, a lot of families who earn their paychecks from SongBird and WRMC. You take this show away from us, and you're responsible for all those pink slips."

Way's face flushed. "I'm not taking anything away!"

"You expect me to believe that? You think I don't know that you've got a meeting next week with that Hollywood bigwig? That this supposed vacation is just you buying some time while you get the ink on that contract?"

Way let go of his sister's hand. "That's not true. None of that is true!"

"I've got sources," Alfie said. "And I'm not going to just stand around and let you make me irrelevant while you keep raking in the big bucks from that deal. Let's see how interested those television people are in you when they find out that *Windy City Gumshoes* has been canceled as of right now."

"What?" Way had taken a step toward his colleague but pulled up short, bafflement—and hurt—on his face. "Why would you do that? How is that not handing out those pink slips?"

"You made it necessary, not me." Alfie tossed the contract onto the faded wooden porch. "The radio show's done. Would have happened regardless, but this way I'm not the only one left holding the bag. You get your share of the pain. No radio means no television. Which means nothing. Not for you, you two-faced—"

"That will be quite enough." Mrs. Folmer rose, though it looked as if standing caused her more than a little discomfort. She managed to translate the pain into a forbidding expression that would have made any mother proud as she leveled it in Alfie's general direction. "You do not come to my home and insult the integrity of my brother. He is a good man. He would do anything for the people he cares about."

Alfie snorted. "Yeah? Well, I hope his integrity keeps him warm at night. Joe and Josie will never see the light of day again, Reynolds. All those merchandising rights, the syndication, the albums? They're mine—and I'm pulling them. You're not going to make another dime from this show. I'll bury it so deep, no Hollywood producer will touch it with a ten-foot pole." He turned on his heel and strode to his car.

"There is no Hollywood producer," Way said wearily.

"Jealousy," Mrs. Folmer pronounced, easing back down into her rocker when the roadster's door slammed shut. "Alfie Paulsen isn't the first man who's let himself be blinded by it. Nor the first to let himself be deceived into disaster by it."

Way let out a long breath and scrubbed a hand over his face. "Showbiz is nasty sometimes. I bet it's a rival show that provided those supposed sources. Everyone knows how afraid Alfie is of television." He focused his gaze on Pearl and Howard again, offering them a small, tired smile. "Sorry, friends. Looks like the auditions in Kansas City are called off."

Howard sighed and held out the script. "Sorry to hear it. It's a real good episode, Way. Real good. We'd have bought the album for sure."

Way waved off the papers. "Keep it. Maybe it'll be a collectible someday," he said with a snort of laughter, clearly doubting it.

"Thanks. I'll practice the lines anyway. Just for the fun of it." Howard slipped his arm around Pearl. Abigail had fallen back to sleep on her shoulder.

Mrs. Folmer let out a long breath of her own. "Well, it looks like now I have to take you in. Seems you're out of work, Weiland."

He laughed. "Seems like. Guess you'll just have to take care of me like you used to do, Lu."

A hint of a smile teased the corners of her mouth. "I guess so."

Howard led Pearl in a pivot to face the stairs again. "We'll get out of your hair."

"I'll walk you. Take the sign down while I'm at it." Way followed them, pausing to pull up the wooden sign about the scripts. "Doesn't look like many people caught on anyway."

He made it sound like a compliment. Pearl sent a sunny, proud smile up at Howard. He winked at her.

They ambled another few steps toward the car, and then Howard paused, turning back to Way, who was apparently one of their new neighbors, at least for a while. "Say...you like bowling, Way?"

Way straightened from where he'd been bent over the sign, a warm smile on his lips. "I do, as a matter of fact. Got a league here?"

"And a team with an opening—if you're interested."

"You know," he said, brushing off his hands, "my schedule just opened up."

✦ Chapter Eighteen ✦

After Lincoln finished explaining contracts to them, he said, "You ladies thinking about writing a book together? Or a screenplay?"

Mary Jane laughed. "Maybe we should. Darla and I can reminisce about the good old days, Robin can back up all our claims with vintage evidence, and Tracy can write it all out for us."

Darla ignored the suggestion in favor of leaning across the table toward Lincoln. "Hold on a second. Didn't you take over the practice of Yancy Hallwell before he retired?"

"Um." Lincoln frowned at what must have seemed like a non sequitur to him, since it sure seemed like one to Tracy, and she knew what they'd been talking about. "I did, yes."

"Does that mean you still have all his old client records?"

Mary Jane sent a narrow-eyed gaze her friend's way. "What are you thinking, Darla?"

"I'm *thinking* that I saw Way Reynolds walking into that office many a time. I worked right across the street back then, remember?" She tapped a finger on the table. "They were friends, so I didn't think much of it, but he was there quite a bit. What if he wasn't just Yancy's friend? What if he was his client? What if he tried at some point to get his rights or whatever from SongBird?"

Tracy set her coffee cup down with a hollow *tap* on the table.

Robin leaned forward, her eyes bright. "That's an interesting theory. It isn't unreasonable to think that he had a lawyer to look over his later publication contracts."

"Later ones?" Darla and Mary Jane both sat up straighter.

"Our grandfather has a box full of books by 'Chance McGee,'" Tracy said. "Just a working theory, but we know he made a living as a writer with a pen name."

"And come to think of it, he must have had a lawyer," Mary Jane said. "For dealing with his estate after he died. If I remember right, he lived on the Folmer farm all those years, didn't he? But he was never the owner of it. It went to Lucy's kids, but they didn't want it. Not until the seventies, when Henry moved home with his kids." She looked at Tracy. "Julie and Tom," she added.

"Not that Tom wanted to hang around Canton." Darla sniffed her opinion of that. "When did Henry pass away? Julie was...was she still in college? I can't remember now."

"It was a year before Way. They both lived out on the farm until then, the widower and his uncle, the bachelor. Remember?"

Darla's eyes went bright with memory. "The two goofballs, that's what we all called them."

Lincoln followed the conversation like someone watching a tennis match, but he interjected now with a shake of his head. "Hate to put a roadblock up on memory lane, ladies, but if I'm following the line of your thinking right, I have to. You all are working on that radio contest, right? Well, I'm sorry to say it doesn't matter if Yancy was Way's lawyer or not. Even if he was, I can't access those files for you. Attorney-client privilege."

Mary Jane scowled. "But he's *dead*."

Lincoln raised his eyebrows. "Does that mean you can go live in his house? Take his car? Transfer money from his account to yours?"

Her scowl deepened. "Of course not."

"Client records belong to the client just like physical property. It's not within a lawyer's purview to disseminate them at will. Upon a client's passing, those files belong to his next of kin."

Tracy met Robin's eyes then Darla's and Mary Jane's. They all smiled, and, in unison, said, "Julie!"

"I can't believe I hadn't thought of this." Julie reached out to shake Lincoln's hand, her smile a little wavery. They all stood in the front room of Lincoln's office, half an hour after Tracy had called her to ask if perhaps the answers about Heath Reynold's legacy could be found in his own legal files.

Tracy hadn't presumed that she and the others would be invited along to the potential discovery, but Julie had insisted. And they hadn't argued.

Julie drew in a long breath and smoothed her hands down her gray slacks. "I honestly didn't look over all the files when he died. Yancy read the will to us, of course."

"And you were the executioner of his estate?" Darla edged forward a little, clearly worried that even now they might not be able to see what was in the files. "You have the legal right to look into these now, right? It's not Tom or his kids?"

Julie's lips twitched into a smile. "It's me. I was the executor. Though I was only twenty-two and newly married. Dealing with my uncle's stuff wasn't high on my list of priorities, so mostly I just accepted the cash he left me, decided to use it to fix up the farm, and then forgot about it." She pressed a hand to her forehead. "I *totally* forgot about it."

Lincoln motioned her toward his office. "While you were en route, I verified that Yancy did indeed still have all the files and I didn't get rid of any of them. You just never know when something's going to come up. I've pulled them all for you."

"All?" Julie followed Lincoln, motioning for Tracy, Robin, Darla, and Mary Jane to come with her.

Well, if she insisted. Tracy exchanged a wink with her cousin and trailed Julie into the room. She'd been in here plenty of times herself, of course, trying to ply information out of Lincoln for her newspaper work. It was a little weird to be here as a tagalong.

"Oh yeah." Lincoln patted a rather large stack of hanging file folders. "Looks like Yancy oversaw all of his publishing contracts for him. I have no idea what else. I just peeked inside the top one here, and that's what it was. You're welcome to review them here, if you like. Or you could take them, if you prefer. I double-checked the will and verified that you're the one entitled to this wealth of information. You can do whatever you like with it."

"Oh my." Julie stared at the stack for a few long moments. It stood a foot high, every inch intimidating, no doubt. After a moment, she looked up at Tracy and company. "Are you ladies busy? It seems I could use some help."

"I'm free!" Darla said, all but rubbing her hands together in anticipation.

Mary Jane rolled her eyes at her. "You already turned your answer in, Darla. I don't know why *you're* so excited."

"Is that silly cruise all you're still thinking about? Good grief, I just want to know!"

"Me too," Tracy said. "And to be fair, Mary Jane…it's really *Julie* finding the answer to her own contest at this point. We wouldn't know a thing without her here."

Julie laughed. "Oh, Tyler's going to get a kick out of this one. That I may have had the answers at my disposal all along. And I tell you what, ladies. I'll put out an official tweak to the rules. Anyone who submits a partially correct answer—at least identifying Heath as Way—will be entered in the drawing. How's that? Does it sound fair?"

Darla obviously thought so, and it only took Mary Jane a moment before she nodded. "Sounds fair to me," she said. "I certainly never would have thought to look for legal files if Darla hadn't mentioned it."

"And Robin and I wouldn't have known who his lawyer was," Tracy said. "See? I told you we'd make a great team, if we put our minds together."

"Well." Julie lifted a few of the files off the pile and handed them to Mary Jane. "How about we take these somewhere more comfortable? If you ladies don't mind a drive out to my house, we'll have lunch and see what we can discover. I'm finished with my classes for the day."

They all agreed and piled into Tracy's and Robin's cars, prepared to follow Julie out to the Folmer farm. Tracy took a moment to check in with Jeff, who was in class but would no doubt call her back afterward. Then she was behind the wheel, on the road she'd traveled just that morning.

Julie's house was as lovely inside as she remembered, each upgrade she'd made designed to highlight the original architecture rather than cover it.

"Oh," Darla said with a happy spin as they entered the foyer. "Lovely! Country chick, isn't that what this is called?"

Mary Jane snorted. "*Chic*, Darla. Not *chick*."

The sparkle in Darla's eyes said she knew very well how the word was pronounced—she should, being in fashion—but that she hadn't been able to resist the joke.

"Let's set up in the living room. That'll be the most comfortable." Julie led the way and dropped the stack of folders onto the coffee table. She took their coats and scarves and purses, deposited them all in a hall closet, and then asked whether they were ready for lunch.

Tracy shook her head. In part because her stomach still wasn't ready for food and in part because she didn't want to wait another minute to crack open those files. The others shook their heads too.

"Okay then. Make yourselves comfortable." Julie smiled and handed them each a file.

The first one Tracy received was full of publishing contracts, which certainly verified her hunch about Way Reynolds being Chance McGee. She didn't bother reading them beyond the first paragraph, establishing what each was for.

The second folder she picked up made her take in a quick breath. "Apparently, he had another pen name too," she announced to the group. "Hugh Grafton." Either he hadn't told Grandpa Howard about that one or Grandpa hadn't collected them or Tracy just hadn't found the box of them yet in the attic.

"And Scott Howard." Mary Jane frowned. "Scott was his agent's last name when he was writing the radio show. And Howard was your grandfather, of course."

"Guess he chose his names with some reasoning behind them," Robin said, smiling.

Tracy bet if she looked through the library or attic, she'd find a collection of Scott Howard books. Assuming they were books. "Novels?"

Mary Jane nodded.

Darla shook her head, her brow creased and her finger tapping a rhythm against her lip. "These aren't. All this stuff is talking about treatments and scripts and show bibles." She looked up. "Somehow I don't think that means special editions of the Scriptures."

"A show bible is all the facts about a television show—character information, setting details, what happened in each episode," Julie said. "It's how writers keep the continuity without contradicting themselves in later seasons." She leaned closer to where Darla had plopped herself at one end of the couch. "What show? I didn't know Uncle Way ever wrote for television."

Darla held out the contract. "*The Magnolia Files.*"

"Whoa." Robin lowered the contract in her hands. "We watched that when I was a teenager! That was Way?"

Darla shrugged. "He's listed as the creator and one of the writers. Looks like there were others too—there's a collaboration section, but it says he'd be the show runner, whatever that is."

"Basically creative director," Julie said, awe in her tone. "Wow. How did I not know this?"

"I guess because he didn't want anyone to know." Tracy picked up another folder—more contracts for the "Scott Howard" pen name. "I wonder if part of his reason for using so many pseudonyms was to keep Alfie Paulsen from claiming infringement? These Scott Howard stories—The Jack and Jill Files. The description sounds pretty similar to Joe and Josie. Sibling investigators solving crimes and mysteries."

"Could be." Julie's brows were knit as she picked up another folder. "This looks promising. 'Reynolds versus SongBird Records.'"

"Really?" Tracy dropped her novel contract, and Robin, Mary Jane, and Darla did the same. They all huddled around Julie, though that required Tracy moving behind the couch and looking over her shoulder.

"Let's see what the date is." Julie paged to the end. When she got there, they all saw the same thing and made little noises of objection.

"It isn't signed," Darla was the first to say.

"But it's dated November 1949. That wouldn't have been all that long after the falling out, assuming it happened around the time the show went off the air," Mary Jane added.

Julie flipped through the rest of the papers in that folder. "No notes about it being filed or sent."

"But plenty of affidavits and statements and whatever else a lawyer calls it when the client lays out his complaint." Tracy leaned into the couch, her gaze trying to take in each page Julie settled on for a moment.

Julie flipped back to the first of the papers. "I'll just read it out loud, okay?"

They all agreed, and Tracy returned to her seat while Julie's voice filled the room. The papers seemed to have been something Way typed up himself, outlining his contract with SongBird Records and WRMC, which Julie paused to dig up and wave in the air. He drew special attention to article two, subheading B, in which he as the creator retained the television subsidiary rights.

"'At the time the contract was signed,'" Julie read, "'television was rare and shows were few, and this felt like a long shot. But I knew at the time that I didn't want the kind of attention that screen actors get, and so I asked to retain those rights because I didn't want someone else deciding for me if I was ready to move into a new realm. By early 1949, however, TV was on the rise and there was definite interest in the television rights to *Windy City Gumshoes*. I considered it, I admit. Not with me playing Joe—I still didn't want that kind of attention—but with me writing. Betty was, at first, all for the idea of transitioning to the screen.

"'But then she got married and started talking about settling down and raising kids, and I knew no one else would play Josie like she did, so I canned the idea. Alfie Paulsen didn't believe me though. Someone, I don't know who, planted the idea in his head that I was trying to go behind his back and transition the show from radio to television and cut him out.

"'Now, the way I see it, had I actually done so, it would have still been profitable for him. Syndication and ratings and merchandising rights would have only increased for the radio show, if a televised version went well. But Alfie didn't see it that way. He was terrified of what the growth of television meant for him and determined to see the worst in me and my motivations. When I asked for a leave of absence to take care of my sister, he thought I was plotting to leave the show for good and sign a television deal. I couldn't convince him otherwise.

"'As witnessed by Howard and Pearl Allen and my sister, Lucy Folmer, Paulsen came out to my sister's farm and promised to bury the show as punishment for this perceived betrayal.'"

Tracy stared at Robin, who stared back at her with her mouth open. Finally, Tracy found her voice. "Our grandparents?"

Julie nodded. "Looks like they were there in connection with the original contest being run, to submit their answer and get a script for the audition."

Well, that at least explained what Grandpa was doing with the script. "Go on."

Julie took a moment to scan the document. "Alfie Paulsen kept his promise—or threat. By the end of the year, albums had been pulled from shelves, merchandise vanished, and syndication stopped. No interviews were given, and when Betty Gardiner gave birth to her first child in October of 1949, everyone just assumed they'd decided to stop recording because of her retirement. Especially since Heath Reynolds was no longer on the radar either." She looked up. "That's the end of this deposition."

Mary Jane reached for another sheet of paper in the folder between them. "Looks like Weiland's official legal complaint was that Paulsen wasn't making good on the 'good faith' portion of the contract that said SongBird would try to make the show a success. So why do you think he decided not to pursue this?"

"Because you can't fight petty without *looking* petty," Darla said. "Besides." She held up another contract. "What did he need with Joe and Josie? This contract is dated December of 1949, for a new series of mystery books. Anyone ever hear of the Lucy Lu detective stories? My mama owned each and every one, and they were some of the first grown-up books I read. Those things were *big* in the fifties."

Tracy wasn't all that familiar with the series, though it rang a bell. And it certainly explained one reason why Way would have decided not to pursue legal measures against Paulsen. He had a new gig, something that kept him busy and successful. Something that led to more deals, across most every form of media.

Almost every form. "So he wrote dozens of novels under several names, he wrote articles and short stories, he even wrote a television show. But he never went back to radio?"

"Maybe he didn't want to risk brushing up against Paulsen again." Julie shrugged, picked up the last folder, and gasped when she opened it.

"What?" the rest of them asked in unison.

"Um." Julie blinked a few times and rubbed a hand over her face. "I, uh...probably should have gone through these files a long time ago. I knew about the accounts Uncle Way left for me, of course. There was enough in them that I completely redid the house and landscaping around here and set up college funds for my kids. Not insubstantial. But these papers show he had stocks and bonds too."

Tracy was dying to ask for details, and it looked like the other ladies itched to peek over Julie's shoulder again too. But they all restrained themselves. And Julie didn't offer more information.

She closed the file, eyes distant, and then offered them a tight smile. "Thank you, ladies. Not sure I would have had the gumption to go through all this on my own. Ready for lunch?"

Tracy still wasn't hungry, but she agreed when the others did. Because it was pretty clear that Julie was done sharing the files, which was absolutely her prerogative.

Pushing herself to her feet, Tracy said, "I think we have our answer about why this has the current generations of Paulsens scared. We have no idea how a judge would have ruled had the case gone to court, but we *do* know that the court of public opinion likely would have weighed in, and it would have been in favor of the stars they knew and loved. And the same holds true today—people would likely champion the creative guy and boo the corporation that tried to squash his legacy and keep him from succeeding with other ventures. Their radio station is on the rocks financially as it is. One negative article could pull their remaining funding."

Julie led them into the kitchen. "That's too bad, though, isn't it? I mean, Alfie was a piece of work, it sounds like. But it isn't his family's fault he acted that way."

"True," Tracy said. "All Ronnie really knows is that he's fighting for his *own* legacy, and it's teetering on the brink of bankruptcy."

"That's really too bad, isn't it?" Robin sighed. "I hate to see the old stuff displaced entirely by the new."

Julie pulled some sandwich fixings from her subzero fridge and smiled. "Maybe it doesn't have to be."

Mary Jane narrowed her eyes. "What are you thinking, Julie?"

Their hostess offered an enigmatic smile. "A solution for everyone, I think. I need to give Ronnie Paulsen a call after lunch. Tracy, will you stick around? Your newspaper connections could come in handy."

Having an idea of where Julie was going, Tracy smiled too. "No problem at all."

Chapter Nineteen

*T*racy looked into the mirror on Saturday evening, turning her head this way and that to observe the waving curls and smiling into the reflection of Amy's face beside her own. "Wow. Where'd you learn how to do finger waves?"

Amy laughed and fussed with a strand of hair Tracy couldn't see at the back of her head. "YouTube. Duh. Hand me one more pin?"

Tracy picked up a hairpin and held it in her open palm for her sister. "I never could have done this. I was just going to put it in a bun and call it a day." She'd been hoping at first that Robin would style her hair, but Robin and Terry had volunteered to help set up the event—transporting some items from her shop as decorations—so the timing hadn't worked out.

"Not on my watch." Amy smoothed, pinned, and then tugged a bit. "There. You, my dear sister, look smashing. Swell. You're the bee's knees. The elephant's instep. The cat's meow. And every other old-timey compliment that's eluding me."

Laughing, Tracy stood from her stool to move over to the full-length mirror. She already had the fascinator in place on her head. Amy had styled the curls around it, and it perfectly complemented the fabulous dress she'd picked up from Darling Darla's the previous day. The last alterations had been done, and it fit like a glove. A sequined, beaded glove that looked like it was straight out of the gilded age of Hollywood. And the pearl-studded long strand Jeff had given her, along with the taper earrings, gave the ensemble the finishing touch. "Definitely turned out pretty well, didn't it?"

"I almost wish I hadn't said I didn't want to go." Amy didn't actually sound too torn up about it though. "Hold on, we missed the hook and eye at the top of the zipper."

Tracy stood still while her sister fastened the hook. "I bet they still have tickets available, if you wanted to ditch your family and tag along."

Amy chuckled. "Much as getting all dressed up is fun, we're pretty set on establishing our Saturday night movie tradition, at least during the winter months."

The plan this week included Amy picking up pizza on her way home from helping Tracy get ready. Which sounded pretty good right about now. "I wonder what the food's going to be at the gala?" Tracy mused at her reflection, turning sideways to see how the dress lay in the back. "Wow, those ladies are good. This dress looks way more expensive than the forty bucks they let me pay for it."

"Forty?" Amy's eyes bulged. "I don't think they even charged you for the fabric, much less the time."

"I tried to object. Darla wouldn't have it. She kept insisting it would be wasted if I didn't take it." She had eventually given up arguing. Sometimes people just needed to be generous, to give a gift—something Darla clearly couldn't resist doing, even in a competition. That meant Tracy's role was to graciously accept and let them be a blessing.

Amy plucked Tracy's bejeweled kitten heels off the ground and held them out. "I expect a whole slew of texts as the evening unfolds.

I want to know who wins the contest and what Julie had up her sleeve with the whole Paulsen thing."

Tracy reached for the first shoe and sat on the edge of the bed to put it on. She'd helped a good bit with "the whole Paulsen thing" yesterday, but she'd also solemnly sworn not to breathe a word of it to anyone but Jeff. Well, and Annette and Eric. They'd had a pretty pivotal role to play too, by agreeing to run her story. "I promise, I'll tell you as soon as I can. It's all good things. Proof of how far the love of family can take you."

Amy handed her the second shoe. "We already knew that lesson." She smiled.

Tracy mirrored it and slid the slingback over her heel. "We did. Though I admit, it was still a nice reminder. Heath's story about sacrificing to take care of his sister and of how God opened so many other doors for him after that. To see how he made a place for himself here and was here for his nephew and his kids when they needed a place to come home to after Julie's mom died."

With a nod, Amy sank down beside her. "Because that's what family does."

"It is." Tracy leaned over to bump their shoulders together. "I'm proud of you, you know. For building your own. Whatever you need as you move into this chapter, I've got your back."

Amy rolled her eyes. "Not to repeat myself, but *duh*. Pretty well established by now, Sis."

Tracy chuckled. "I know, but…I admit, I've had a few thoughts these last two weeks, wondering how I still fit in, now that your house is brimming. I don't want to impose, but I also don't want to give you *too* much space." She shrugged.

Amy chuckled. "You have no need to worry. If I go a few days without hearing from you, you can bet I'll be calling to harass you or ask advice about something—or *give* advice about something. Like, for instance, that watch. You are not allowed to wear your fitness watch to a gala."

"Oops!" She'd meant to take it off earlier so that the lines it left on her wrist would fade, but apparently, she'd forgotten. With a laugh, she took it off, tossed it onto her dresser, and got out the silver bracelet watch that had been Grandma Pearl's. "Better?"

"So much better." Amy helped her fasten it after she'd wound and set it, then looked at its face. "And on that note, I'd better go. Don't forget those updates!"

"I won't, I promise."

She walked her sister down and out through the kitchen door. Jeff, who'd been ready an hour ago, sat at the kitchen table with Wednesday's newspaper open in front of him. "Bye, Amy," he called after her.

"Have fun!" Amy called. "And you'll be adding a thank-you after you actually take a gander at your lovely wife."

He did so, eyes going wide when she spun to give him the full effect. "Yowza. Looking good, dollface," he said in an exaggerated mobster drawl.

Tracy laughed and struck a pose. "Thanks. You clean up pretty good yourself." He wore a black pinstripe suit and even had a striking white fedora to pair with it. "We're going to be quite the handsome couple."

"Got that right. Shall we? I already let Sadie out one last time."

"I'm ready."

The drive to the hotel ballroom didn't take very long, and soon Jeff had presented their tickets with a flourish, Tracy had checked her wrap, and they followed the swing music into the beautifully appointed chamber. Tables were set up for the dinner portion, but a large dance floor had been left open, and Tracy laughed in delight when she spotted both Darla and Mary Jane dancing with their husbands.

"Those cats sure cut a mean rug," Jeff said in her ear, following their gaze.

She chuckled and shook her head. "Are you going to talk like that all night?"

"Maybe. I studied up."

The current song reached its cadence and came to an end, and Tracy and Jeff added their applause and whistles for both the live band and the dancers.

Darla spotted her, waved, and trotted toward them, her husband in tow. "There you are! Robin and her husband already got us a table. As long as you don't mind rubbing elbows with that Mary Jane Shoemaker," she added with a wink.

Tracy had a feeling she'd be laughing all night. "I think I can handle it." Though her good mood hiccupped a little when she spotted Ronnie Paulsen standing just inside the door, a lovely sixtysomething woman at his side, and a younger couple right behind them.

She dropped her things at the table Darla pointed her to but then tugged Jeff toward the door. Robin and Terry must have spotted them, because they appeared on the other side of Jeff and followed along. The Paulsens had come inside by a few more steps but hadn't made any move to find a table or talk to anyone.

"Our guests of honor, I take it?" Jeff said as they closed the distance between them.

"Yep." Tracy made sure to keep her smile bright. "I'm glad they came. I was afraid they wouldn't."

"For good reason," Robin muttered.

She hummed her agreement but said no more, since they were close enough now that the Paulsens had noticed their approach. The other three made no move, but Ronnie, after a few blinks in which he was clearly trying to place her, donned his pleasant mask of a smile and stepped forward, hand outstretched.

"Tracy Doyle! I barely recognized you."

She laughed and shook his hand. "Far cry from my ponytail and jeans, I know. This is my husband, Jeff, and my cousin Robin and her husband, Terry. Everyone, this is Ronnie Paulsen, from the radio station in Chicago."

Ronnie introduced his wife, son, and daughter-in-law.

Before an awkward silence could even think of descending, Tracy beamed another smile at them. "We're so glad you could come! Julie especially. We all want you to know that we really respect how you're keeping your family's legacy alive, and we want to do all we can to help with that. We promise her uncle's story won't in any way hinder that."

Ronnie glanced at his wife. "That's what Julie said when she called, though I admit I was dubious. I've seen the records and my father's notes on the old contract. I know... Well, I know he cut off his nose to spite his own face with how he treated Heath and the whole *Windy City Gumshoes* franchise. He acted out of fear, and he paid for it. The SongBird Records studio closed in 1951, you know."

Tracy nodded. "He did. But that's no reason for *you* to fear. You're not your father, and even if you were, well…" She exchanged a grin with Jeff. "Julie has a surprise for you. Turns out Heath didn't hold a grudge, so why would his niece?"

Mrs. Paulsen smiled and squeezed her husband's arm. "See, sweetheart? I told you."

Tracy waved them along. "Come on, you can take the table next to ours. And then you can flaunt your stuff on the dance floor."

Finally smiling with genuine warmth, the quartet of Paulsens followed them into the party.

For the first hour, they used the table as a base of operations—a place to hold their handbags and plates as they moved from buffet tables to conversations to dance floor and back again. The food—finger foods and hors d'oeuvres—was delicious and unique, and Tracy might have snuck a few more stuffed dates than she should have. They laughed and chatted with old friends and new and marveled over and again at the talent of the musicians and vocalists.

At eight o'clock, Ken stepped up to the microphone, clapped for the set the band had just wrapped up, and then said, "Okay, guys and gals, if you'll all make your way to your seats, it's time for the chitchat portion of the evening."

Tracy and Jeff joined the tide of guests ebbing off the floor. Seeing Julie standing by the stage, she had to smile and glance over at Ronnie and his wife. If she wasn't mistaken, a bit of nervousness had crept back into Ronnie's posture.

It wouldn't last. Not for long.

Ken introduced Julie as the sponsor of the contest, which earned a loud round of applause and a few gasps of surprise

from people who apparently hadn't made all the family connections yet.

Julie stepped up to the mic with a wave, her cheeks looking
flushed but her smile bright. She wore a classic black dress in the
style of the forties, her hair in a victory roll. "Thank you all so much
for coming. Thank you for participating in the *Turn Back the Dial*
contest. And most of all, thank you for being such wonderful friends
and neighbors and such wonderful examples for us all."

She reached into the beaded handbag looped over her wrist and
pulled out a few sheets of paper. "I'm going to announce the results
of the contest in just a few minutes. The rules stated that everyone
who turned in the correct answer to both questions would be entered
to win, but I had to accept partial answers as correct when it became
clear that the full answer I was looking for couldn't be found by
anyone but, well, *me*."

The audience laughed and applauded.

Julie ducked her head. "I know, I know. Had I just looked through
my own files *first*…but alas. And honestly, I'm glad it worked out this
way. It showed me something I think we all sometimes forget—that
the love we show each other, our families, and our neighbors is the
love of God lived out in the world today. Every time we work together,
every time we build each other up, every time we make a sacrifice for
the people next to us, we are acting like Christ."

She lifted the paper. "But I'm not here to preach. I'm here to
share with you a bit of my uncle's legacy. Most of you who were
around in the eighties or before knew him as Weiland Reynolds.
Uncle Way was an icon in this town because of his generosity of
spirit, openness of heart, and good humor. But what most of his

neighbors never knew was that he was an icon in the entertainment world too—just not under his real name. Some people knew him as Heath Reynolds…or as Chance McGee. He was Scott Howard. And he was Hugh Grafton."

A series of surprised noises rippled and grew around the room so that Julie had to pause and wait for them to die back down. Clearly, many people here had heard of at least one of Way's pseudonyms. Even now, so many years later, his mysteries were known and lauded as some of the classics of the genre.

Julie aimed a smile toward the front table, where her family sat—including a teenage boy. He and the teenage girl next to him seemed to be having a blast, despite being the only people there under twenty. "Uncle Way gave up a career at its height to move to Canton and care for his sister, Lucy, who was dying from organ failure caused by diabetes. It was a hard time for anyone with the disease. It wasn't an immediate death sentence as it had once been, but treatment was in its infancy. My grandma Lucy went blind and faced amputation, but she knew she wasn't alone. She had family. And I know if she's looking down from heaven today, she's seeing her family, generations later, and is so proud. I know she's loving each one of us and cheering us on. I know that she's so proud of the Type 1 Warrior in our family today, ready to charge after his dreams."

Carson, his face red, ducked his head. But he was grinning.

"Grandma Lucy was a warrior, and her brother was an inspiration. Because, though Uncle Way made that sacrifice, it wasn't the end of his career. It was just the beginning. It set his feet on the path he walked the rest of his life with the greatest of joys. He loved writing. I remember coming into his room while he was at his typewriter and seeing a smile on his face as he created worlds I couldn't begin to understand at the time. But I understand now. And I am so, so proud of all he accomplished. Of the legacy he built. He chose to make it an invisible castle, a silent testimony, a quiet fame. He kept it all secret because he didn't want people to confuse who he was for what he did. He didn't want to be known and defined by his circumstances. And he wasn't. He was known and defined by his faith and its constant demonstration."

She smoothed out the paper she held and searched the crowd, her gaze finally stopping at the Paulsens' table. "We have in our midst tonight a few very special guests. Ronnie Paulsen, his wife, Carrie, his son, Jake, and his daughter-in-law, Mercy. Ronnie is the son of my uncle's first producer, Alfie Paulsen. Alfie was the one who first saw Way's talent, who first gave him a shot. He's the one who brought *Windy City Gumshoes* to the airwaves. Ronnie, would you please stand up?"

Ronnie stood, looking a little uncomfortable as he waved.

"As is too often the case in life, Uncle Way and Alfie had a misunderstanding and parted ways in 1949. But as I was going through my uncle's files yesterday, I found this. A copy of a letter. According to his notes, he sent it to your father, Ronnie, in 1980. I have no idea whether it opened a dialogue between the two men at the time, but I do know it spoke to my heart, and I hope it speaks to yours."

She cleared her throat and began to read. "'Dear Alfie, Well, old friend, a lot of years have gone by. A lot of water has flowed under the bridges of our lives. I look back on that silly argument on my sister's front porch, and I wonder why. Why did we let that be the end of our friendship? Why did we let fear and frustration and anger ruin what we'd built through trust and goodwill and the power of dreams? I don't know.

"'But I do know this—what the enemy meant for evil, God used for good. He used it to set me on the path He wanted me on, the path where I have flourished and known true happiness. He used it to encourage Betty and Sam to focus on their family instead of her career, which I know she hasn't regretted for even a day. And I hope and pray that maybe it played a role in leading you too toward happiness. I can't tell you how glad I was to hear that you finally got married. And to Maxine! She waited a long time for you, you know. I pray you bring each other every joy.

"'I also pray that you'll forgive me for any distress I caused you. I want you to know that I forgive you for the pain I felt. At the time, I thought all that mattered was who was right and who was wrong. But you know, I don't think that's actually all that important. What matters is that in each moment, we choose the good. We choose the beautiful. We choose what's true. And that's this: I owe you everything, Alfie. Everything. If you hadn't taken a shot on me, I don't know where I'd be. I'm grateful. And I'm humbled. And I'm honored to have gotten to count you as a friend in this life.'"

When Julie stopped reading, applause filled the air again. When Tracy looked over, she saw a smile on Ronnie's face and a tear on his cheek.

Julie wiped at her own tears. "All right. Enough of the sappy stuff. Now, the contest."

More cheers and hoots.

She leafed through her papers. "Though there were a dozen entries, we ended up with only four people who came to me with the correct solution to the puzzle. Or with as much as could be found without breaking into my uncle's lawyer's office—which I don't recommend, just for the record." A ripple of laughter. "I was going to draw the winner from those four names. But…" She smiled at the front table. "As it happens, my uncle left me a bigger inheritance than I'd thought. And I can't imagine a better use for it than honoring the people—the friendships—of this town. So my husband and I have decided that all four of these couples win the prize."

This time the gasps turned to shouts and squeals, especially from Tracy's table, where Darla and Mary Jane had both reached for each other and had their arms entwined.

"So our winners are…"

The band's drummer played a drumroll, which brought out another burst of laughter.

"Darla and Ike Franklin, Mary Jane and Pat Shoemaker, Nancy and Kevin Kramer, and Tracy and Jeff Doyle. Come on up here, all of you!"

"What?" Tracy jerked when Julie read off their names, her gaze clashing with Jeff's. "But we told her to take us out…. I thought…"

He laughed and pulled her to her feet. "I guess she figured we'd turned in our answer to her before that second part was made known—which you *did* help her figure out, honey."

Robin all but pushed Tracy up. "Jeff's right. Don't argue."

How could she, when Darla and Mary Jane pulled them toward the stage with laughter and bouncing steps? She felt like she was just along for the ride—and it was a fun one, so that was fine.

Julie hugged all of them, and her husband came up to hand them each an envelope—and, hilariously, a sailor's hat.

"We should all go together," Darla said. "Even you, Pat. No getting out of it."

Pat Shoemaker held out a hand in defeat. "Fine, fine. Guess I'm due for a real vacation."

Mary Jane looked she might float off the stage.

The band struck up a rousing tune, Julie ordered the winning couples onto the floor, and Tracy smiled until her cheeks hurt as Jeff swung her around. The looks on the other couples' faces were priceless. All courtesy of a creative man who hadn't written a word in decades yet whose words had cast a spirit of gratitude over everyone at the gala.

She saw Ronnie making his way toward Julie as the winners danced. After Julie's wave of invitation, Ken joined them, and they seemed to be discussing something. She couldn't think of anything that would have made Ken leap away from them like he did and smile quite that big. Not until he took the microphone after the song was done.

"Well, folks, this is something. This is really, really something. Ronnie Paulsen, the rights-holder to the original *Windy City Gumshoes* show, along with Julie Missenden, the rights-holder to the writings of Heath Reynolds, have just announced—" Ken stepped back, heaved a breath, and looked over toward the two in question again.

Ronnie and Julie were both smiling.

Ken did too. "The show is finally going to be completed! The last, promised episode of the unfinished season will be produced right here in our own studios, and *you*, our friends and families, are invited to audition. That one episode will air here and in Chicago…

and if it's well received, we'll run the whole season. And who knows, after that? Maybe Joe and Josie will be given new life! It seems that Way, as Heath, wrote a couple more seasons just to get the ideas out during his first days in Canton, and Julie is willing to license it to WRMC if the audience approves!"

Tracy couldn't predict how the general radio audience would react, but the audience in Canton made their approval well known.

Tracy leaned into Jeff, clapping as loudly as anyone. "Here's to good ratings, right?"

He sent her a wink. "You said it, dollface."

Dear Reader,

When my husband and I made the decision to move back to our hometown of Cumberland, Maryland, we knew it would mean giving up a lot of the culture that Annapolis offered. But one of our first weekends home again, he came to my mom's (where we were staying for Christmas) after a day of working on our new-to-us house and said, "Turn on the radio! To 91.9."

We turned on the set in my mom's kitchen, and I gasped. Big band music spilled out! It was my favorite—because that's just the kind of twenty-two-year-old I was. I started dancing around my mom's living room with our three-month-old baby, and my husband stood there, grinning, happy to have found this treasure for me. The program still airs every Friday night. We turn it on nearly every week, and my kids grew up dancing to it. I have some precious, priceless memories linked to that. The local program is called *Jukebox Friday Night*, run by Ken Heath—a local pastor with a passion for the good old days of radio. In more recent years, he's added *Turn Back the Dial* to the lineup after the music, where he airs old radio dramas, comedies, and mysteries. Obviously those two shows were what inspired me to insert some classic radio drama into the stories from Grandma's attic. (I wrote him to let him know. He was pretty enthusiastic about the idea.)

Though I'm a big fan of new methods of reaching people with story or art, I'm also a big fan of preserving the old ways and enjoying them for the classics they are. Whether it's old music, old shows, or old books, there's more than just charm to be found—there's the very history on which our media today stands. Whatever you most enjoy in music and story, I hope this little peek into an era too often overlooked brings a smile to your face…and makes you want to turn back the dial.

Signed,
Roseanna M. White

About The Author

Roseanna M. White is a bestselling, Christy Award-winning author who has long claimed that words are the air she breathes. When not writing fiction, she's homeschooling her two kids, managing a publishing company with her husband, designing book covers, and pretending her house will clean itself. Roseanna is the author of a slew of historical novels that span several continents and thousands of years. Spies and war and mayhem always seem to find their way into her books...to offset her real life, which is blessedly ordinary.

COLLECTIBLES *From* GRANDMA'S ATTIC

Radio

*W*hile we still have plenty of radio programing today, modern listeners may not be aware of the rich past linked to those old console sets we see mostly on television these days. Radio technology was a new creation for the twentieth century and was in fact banned from civilian use during the First World War. In the Roaring Twenties, though, radio came into its own. Stations sprang up, broadcasting sporting events, the opera season, popular music, and scripted shows.

As the country rebounded from the war, radios began appearing in every home, and they often became the focal point of the living room. That's why you'll find those beautiful wooden creations hiding away in attics and yard sales today. Families would gather around the radio in the evenings, children would listen to educational programing while their parents did chores, and parents would listen to mysteries, dramas, and comedy hours after the little ones were tucked into bed.

The golden age of radio lasted only until the 1950s, however. In the course of five years, television began to dominate the scene, and it became the new, preferred medium for Americans' entertainment. While radio persisted and still does, it took a back seat, and radio shows gradually got canceled. Radios themselves were no longer a focal point of decor and, as technology allowed, grew smaller and less obtrusive.

Even so, they haven't given up their role entirely, and collectors still refurbish and bring new life to the old designs.

Double Chocolate Cookies

Ingredients:

- ½ cup (1 stick) butter, softened
- ½ cup granulated sugar
- ½ cup packed brown sugar
- 1 egg at room temperature
- 1 teaspoon vanilla extract
- 1 cup all-purpose flour
- ⅔ cup cocoa powder
- 1 teaspoon baking soda
- ⅛ teaspoon salt
- 1 tablespoon milk
- 1¼ cups semi-sweet chocolate chips

Instructions:

Note! This recipe works best if the dough is chilled overnight.

In a large bowl with an electric mixer, beat together butter and sugars until light and fluffy, about 2 to 3 minutes. Add egg (having it at room temperature will keep it from making the butter hard again) and vanilla and beat until combined.

In a separate bowl, whisk together flour, cocoa powder, baking soda, and salt. Slowly mix into butter and sugar mixture until combined. Dough will be thick. Add milk. Finally, stir in chocolate chips.

Refrigerate dough for at least three hours, or overnight.

When ready to bake, remove dough from fridge and let sit for 10 to 20 minutes. Preheat oven to 350 and line cookie sheets with parchment paper or baking mats. Scoop dough into large balls, using about a tablespoon and a half for each ball. Position them at least two inches apart on cookie sheet.

Bake 9 to 11 minutes. Edges should appear set, but centers will still look soft. Remove from oven and let cool for 5 minutes then remove them to racks to cool completely. Store at room temperature for a week…if they last that long.

*Read on for a sneak peek of another exciting book
in the Secrets from Grandma's Attic series!*

A Marathon of Kindness

By D'Ann Mateer

"Mom." Seven-year-old Jana tossed her backpack onto Amy Allen's desk in her classroom. "Guess what we learned about today?"

Natalie—Amy's stepdaughter and Jana's best friend—stood next to Jana, looking as if she would explode with the news before Jana got the words out.

"I can't imagine," Amy said, leaning forward, hands anchored on her slightly bent knees.

"Money!" Jana's fists clenched then rose into the air.

Amy stood up straight, hands on her hips, eyebrows lifted. "Well, now. That *is* exciting."

"Can we count some money when we get home? Please, please, please!" Natalie squeezed her eyes shut as she pleaded.

"Please, what?" Matt, Amy's sixth-grade son, strode into the room. Colton, his best friend and Amy's new stepson, walked in with him.

Despite the girls' excitement, Amy's attention latched on to the boys. Their smug expressions put her on alert.

Jana spun to face the boys. "We're learning how to count money in math."

Matt and Colton met each other's eyes and grinned. Matt shrugged. "Baby stuff."

Uh-oh.

Amy inserted herself between the boys and the girls. Sure enough, Jana's cheeks splotched red, and tears welled in her eyes. And Natalie? A storm cloud, ready to burst. Amy hadn't imagined that one of the most common issues they'd face thus far with a blended family would be the girls versus the boys. But that seemed to be the case more often than not lately.

She faced Matt and Colton. "Enough," she said, her voice low and filled with teacher authority. At least Colton had the decency to hang his head. Matt simply avoided her eyes. Ashamed, she felt sure, but not as willing to admit it. If Miles had been confronting them, the boys' reactions would likely have been reversed. They both tried so hard to please their new parent.

Amy returned her attention to the girls. Natalie was comforting Jana, both of them wiping tears away. Amy sighed. *Oh, the drama.* She needed to diffuse this and provide a distraction. Otherwise, the girls would stay mad at the boys until—well, until they had something better to think about.

Money. Money. Money. Amy rubbed her forehead like a genie's lamp, praying for an idea to both assuage and excite the girls.

The image of a large glass jug filled with coins jumped into her head. Great-grandpa Nicholas's coin jar.

Tracy hadn't gotten rid of it. But she had stowed it away somewhere, fearful her small grandchildren would swallow a coin or stuff one in a nostril.

Amy whipped out her phone and shot off a text to her sister.

Great-grandpa's coin jar?

Hm. Why?

Girls studying money at school.

Got it. I'll pull it out for Sunday.

Amy sent a thumbs-up emoji then dropped her phone into her purse. The distraction wouldn't do its job today, but maybe just the promise would be enough.

"Okay, girls. Aunt Tracy will have a huge jar of coins for you to count on Sunday afternoon after dinner."

Both of their faces lit with excitement. Then the squealing began. And the jumping up and down.

Amy fought the desire to roll her eyes. A person would think she'd offered them a trip to Disney World instead of the opportunity to add up pennies, nickels, dimes, and quarters.

Whatever made them happy.

At least for this moment.

"Troops, to the car!" Amy pointed to the hallway. The boys ambled out, and the girls followed. Amy took the rear, goading the girls along like in those videos of border collies with errant lambs. Finally, they were loaded up and on their way home.

Not her home, she still had to remind herself. Miles's family home that he'd bought when he moved back to Canton. *Their* home. Together. With these four hooligans.

She smiled into the rearview mirror. Not only had God given her Matt and Jana through adoption, now He'd given her Natalie and Colton through marriage. Gratitude threatened to overwhelm her every single day.

It didn't take long to arrive at the grand Victorian home. What an upgrade this was to the always-needs-something-fixed house she shared with the kids when she was single. It was charming, but this home was stately. She could hardly believe it was her address now. She turned into the driveway. Matt and Colton hopped out to open the garage door. She drove inside, where she and the girls got out of the car.

The boys had already disappeared into the house, using the hidden key. But before Amy could shepherd the girls inside, the boys came racing out again.

"Mom!" Matt yelled. "There's a package on the porch! And it's heavy!" He tugged Colton's shirt sleeve, and they both disappeared into the house again.

What has Miles ordered now? Amy shook her head. Ever since the wedding, it felt like a new package appeared on the porch about every day. Everything from frames for wedding pictures to matching bedroom linens the girls had talked him into. She loved how excited Miles was about their life together, but seriously? This had to stop.

Amy hustled in front of the girls. They'd gotten distracted in the backyard, searching for new leaves on the still-bare tree near their playhouse. She slid her satchel and purse onto the island in the kitchen and kept going through to the front of the house. The door stood open, both boys peering at a box wrapped in the most unusual wrapping paper Amy had ever seen.

Wedding wrapping paper, for sure, but not traditional paper. Instead of elegant silver or gold, bright colors swirled across the black background. *Congratulations* was written in a font normally reserved for words like *Groovy* or *Far Out.*

"We've got it, Mom." Matt put his hands under one end of the box, Colton the other. Then they carried it into the living room and set it in front of the fireplace.

"Are you going to open it now or wait for Dad?" Colton asked.

"Now! Now!" the girls squealed in concert.

Amy shook her head. "Your dad will be home soon. I can wait."

The girls drooped in disappointment, and Amy swallowed a giggle. They were a mess, but oh, how they made her laugh. "Until then, it's homework time."

"On a Friday?" Matt looked incredulous.

Amy set her hand on her son's head. "If you get it done now, you won't be scrambling on Sunday night."

He pleaded with his eyes, and she chuckled. "Okay, then. Snack time."

He and Colton disappeared into the kitchen. The girls followed. Amy examined the package. She couldn't find a card on the outside. Who in the world could it be from?

Moments later, she heard a car turn into the driveway. The girls shot out the kitchen door, and once Miles stepped foot in the house, they danced around him, talking over each other.

Bright with suppressed laughter, his eyes met Amy's over their daughters' heads. Amy's heart lodged in her throat. Oh, how she loved this man!

"Okay, okay." He raised his hands, and the girls stilled. "If I understand this correctly, there is a wedding gift in the living room."

Amy crossed her arms and smirked at her husband. "You'd think it was for them, the way they're carrying on."

Miles laughed, took two steps past the girls, and planted a kiss on Amy's lips.

"Welcome home," she murmured. They shared a silent laugh.

"Hey, Dad." The boys spoke in tandem as they came into the kitchen.

Miles greeted them then raised his eyebrows at Amy. She shrugged. She didn't believe for a moment that Matt and Colton weren't as excited and curious about the gift as their sisters. They just covered it in eleven-year-old-boy indifference.

"Shall we, Mrs. Anderson?" Miles held out his hand to Amy.

"We shall." She put her hand in his, and they walked, prim and proper, into the living room until they reached the hideously wrapped box.

"Um…" Miles's unspoken question lingered.

Amy opened her mouth, but it was Natalie who spoke.

"Isn't that the coolest wrapping paper, Dad?"

Miles's eyes met Amy's. She hoped he could read her suggestion.

"Yes, honey. Very cool." Amy breathed a sigh of relief. Not only did she fear his true feelings on the matter would hurt his daughter, but she also suspected any comments they made about it would eventually reach the gift giver. And she didn't want to hurt that person's feelings either. Whoever they were.

Amy knelt in front of the box. "Let's get this show on the road. Your dad and I have pizza to prepare!"

The kids scooted away, and Miles closed the gap behind her. Amy found the taped seam on one end and ripped into the vintage wrapping paper. The brown box beneath had no markings. It didn't appear to be new, though the tape keeping it shut was clearly a recent application. Miles fished his keys out of his pocket and handed them to Amy. Using the sharp edge of the longest one, she slit the tape. Then she opened the flaps and removed the packing paper. She stared, wide-eyed, at the divider with twelve slots. In each slot was a wrapped object of some kind.

Miles reached over her shoulder and lifted one of the wrapped pieces. Carefully, he removed paper and then bubble wrap, until a goblet-style glass sat in his hand.

"Glasses?" Amy scrunched her nose.

Who would give them drinking glasses? And a dozen, at that? It wasn't as if she and Miles were young, setting up their first home. In fact, they'd been getting rid of duplicates, not adding new things.

He held it up for her to inspect. Sleek stem and bowl. An intricate diamond pattern cut deep into what appeared to be heavy glass, fading to an etch near the rim. Sparkling clear.

Amy touched the delicate vessel. "I wonder who sent these?"

"I'll find the card!" Jana shouted as she lunged for the box, Natalie close behind.

"Stop!" Amy's teacher voice froze them before their hands hit the fragile treasures. "Miles, will you look for a card, please?"

He handed Amy the glass and carefully lifted the eleven others before replacing them in their cocoons. He even removed all the padding around the edge of the box.

"Nothing," he said, shaking his head.

Amy studied the unwrapped goblet again. Could it be...

She held it up to the light, turning it this way and that. She'd learned from helping her cousin Robin at her antique store that the more famous crystal companies stamped their work. And then it caught the light, the faintly etched word on the bottom of the glass.

"Waterford," she said. So, not an insignificant gift. She put the glass on the mantel, out of reach of curious hands. "I'll call Tracy and Robin. Maybe together we can figure out who to thank for such an extravagant gift."

Miles's expression changed, reminding her of Colton's when he'd struck out with the bases loaded last summer.

Amy cocked her head. "What?"

"I thought—never mind." His smile returned. "Guess we need to get dinner started."

"Dinner! Yes!" Matt fist-bumped Colton before they headed upstairs.

Amy wanted to think they'd listen to her and get their weekend homework done now, but she had too much experience with kids to believe that.

"Girls, want to help with the pizzas?" she asked instead.

"Mom." Jana put her hands on her hips, suddenly seventeen instead of seven. "We have to pick out the movie we're going to watch after dinner. It's our turn to choose."

The girls went to the collection of DVDs they would be allowed to choose from. Then Natalie turned to Amy. "And don't forget, we need to practice counting money this weekend."

Amy nodded. "I know. I promise Aunt Tracy will have a huge jar ready for you on Sunday."

She noticed Miles staring at the wedding gift, but something told her he wasn't actually seeing the box full of crystal.

"Ready to make some pizza?" she asked, wrapping her arms around his waist.

His ready grin made her heart happy.

"You bet." He kissed the tip of her nose. "Let's get 'er done."

Saturday brought a mix of responsibilities and rest. But as Amy tackled her morning chores and later curled into a chair for some afternoon reading, her mind continued to wander to the Waterford glasses.

She'd texted both Tracy and Robin to alert them to a new mystery, but for some reason neither appeared eager to help. She pondered that as Miles and the boys watched Mizzou—University of Missouri—basketball on TV. Usually, her sister and cousin were eager for any new puzzle to solve. So why their lack of enthusiasm now?

She shifted on the sofa beside Miles. His arm snaked around her waist and drew her close even though his eyes didn't leave the game for a moment. Lately, she'd realized living with a man and almost-adolescent boys took more getting used to than she had imagined. But he clearly wanted her near. And that made her happy.

Now if she could only figure out who the mysterious gift giver was.

When the final game buzzer sounded, the guys groaned. A loss. Not even close. Matt and Colton asked for permission to ride their bikes to the park. After they were off, Miles raised his eyes to the ceiling.

"What do you think the girls are doing up there?"

Amy smiled. "Probably making up worlds from their imagination. Don't boys do the same thing?" She elbowed him gently in the ribs.

"Yes, but we usually let our imaginations run wild outdoors. Or we did until video games were invented. Then the worlds were created for us."

Amy immediately sobered. "That's really sad. I hate that children's imaginations have been replaced with prepackaged play."

"That's one of the big reasons I moved us to Canton. Obviously, Colton has video games. But here it's easier to say, 'Go outside and play' than it was in Chicago."

"True." Amy snuggled closer to her husband. "Which makes it nice for us. The boys at the park. The girls playing upstairs."

He smiled at her before they shared a kiss. Contentment washed over Amy. Married life might be an adjustment after decades of singleness, but it was worth the effort.

Suddenly, footsteps pounded on the stairs, high-pitched voices following.

"Mom? Can you ask Aunt Tracy if we can start counting her coins now? Please? We can't wait until tomorrow!" Jana bounced on her toes while Natalie muttered "pretty please" over and over again.

Miles shook his head and lurched off the sofa. "It's up to you, Amy. I have to mow the lawn."

Amy considered the girls' pleas. Who could resist those cherubic faces?

Not her.

"Okay, I'll ask. But she might be busy today, so don't get your hopes up."

"Yessssss," they cheered in stereo as they high-fived each other.

Amy called her sister. She'd get an answer more quickly that way than with a text.

"Hey, Amy! What's up?"

"I have two eager girls here. Any chance they can sort some coins today rather than waiting until tomorrow?"

Tracy laughed. "How can I say no to children who want to do schoolwork on a Saturday afternoon? Bring them over. There'll be plenty to keep them busy both today and tomorrow. Maybe even from now until they graduate!"

Amy chuckled. According to Grandma Pearl, her father, Great-grandpa Nicholas, had been putting coins in that jar since he was sixteen, which was sometime before World War I.

"Got it. We'll be over in a few minutes." Amy nodded Tracy's answer to the girls. They raced to find their shoes.

"We'll be here. I'll have Jeff lug the jar into my reading room upstairs. That way I can close the door between today and tomorrow and we won't disturb their progress."

"Perfect." They said goodbye and disconnected. Amy slipped into her shoes, which sat by the back door. March had come in the day before like a lamb, but even with the sun shining the air still felt like winter. Amy shivered before sliding her arms into her coat. She was definitely ready for spring.

A Note from the Editors

We hope you enjoyed another exciting volume in the Secrets from Grandma's Attic series, published by Guideposts. For over seventy-five years, Guideposts, a nonprofit organization, has been driven by a vision of a world filled with hope. We aspire to be the voice of a trusted friend, a friend who makes you feel more hopeful and connected.

By making a purchase from Guideposts, you join our community in touching millions of lives, inspiring them to believe that all things are possible through faith, hope, and prayer. Your continued support allows us to provide uplifting resources to those in need. Whether through our communities, websites, apps, or publications, we inspire our audiences, bring them together, and comfort, uplift, entertain, and guide them. Visit us at guideposts.org to learn more.

We would love to hear from you. Write us at Guideposts, P.O. Box 5815, Harlan, Iowa 51593 or call us at (800) 932-2145. Did you love *Turn Back the Dial*? Leave a review for this product on guideposts.org/shop. Your feedback helps others in our community find relevant products.

Find inspiration, find faith, find Guideposts.

Shop our best sellers and favorites at

guideposts.org/shop

Or scan the QR code to go directly to our Shop

Savannah Secrets

Welcome to Savannah, Georgia, a picture-perfect Southern city known for its manicured parks, moss-covered oaks, and antebellum architecture. Walk down one of the cobblestone streets, and you'll come upon Magnolia Investigations. It is here where two friends have joined forces to unravel some of Savannah's deepest secrets. Tag along as clues are exposed, red herrings discarded, and thrilling surprises revealed. Find inspiration in the special bond between Meredith Bellefontaine and Julia Foley. Cheer the friends on as they listen to their hearts and rely on their faith to solve each new case that comes their way.

The Hidden Gate
A Fallen Petal
Double Trouble
Whispering Bells
Where Time Stood Still
The Weight of Years
Willful Transgressions

Season's Meetings
Southern Fried Secrets
The Greatest of These
Patterns of Deception
The Waving Girl
Beneath a Dragon Moon
Garden Variety Crimes
Meant for Good
A Bone to Pick
Honeybees & Legacies
True Grits
Sapphire Secret
Jingle Bell Heist
Buried Secrets
A Puzzle of Pearls
Facing the Facts
Resurrecting Trouble
Forever and a Day

Mysteries of Martha's Vineyard

Priscilla Latham Grant has inherited a lighthouse! So with not much more than a strong will and a sore heart, the recent widow says goodbye to her lifelong Kansas home and heads to the quaint and historic island of Martha's Vineyard, Massachusetts. There, she comes face-to-face with adventures, which include her trusty canine friend, Jake, three delightful cousins she didn't know she had, and Gerald O'Bannon, a handsome Coast Guard captain—plus head-scratching mysteries that crop up with surprising regularity.

A Light in the Darkness

Like a Fish Out of Water

Adrift

Maiden of the Mist

Making Waves

Don't Rock the Boat

A Port in the Storm

Thicker Than Water

Swept Away

Bridge Over Troubled Waters

Smoke on the Water

Shifting Sands

Shark Bait

Seascape in Shadows

Storm Tide

Water Flows Uphill

Catch of the Day

Beyond the Sea

Wider Than an Ocean

Sheeps Passing in the Night

Sail Away Home

Waves of Doubt

Lifeline

Flotsam & Jetsam

Just Over the Horizon

Miracles & Mysteries of Mercy Hospital

Four talented women from very different walks of life witness the miracles happening around them at Mercy Hospital and soon become fast friends. Join Joy Atkins, Evelyn Perry, Anne Mabry, and Shirley Bashore as, together, they solve the puzzling mysteries that arise at this Charleston, South Carolina, historic hospital— rumored to be under the protection of a guardian angel. Come along as our quartet of faithful friends solve mysteries, stumble upon a few of the hospital's hidden and forgotten passageways, and discover historical treasures along the way! This fast-paced series is filled with inspiration, adventure, mystery, delightful humor, and loads of Southern charm!

Where Mercy Begins
Prescription for Mystery
Angels Watching Over Me
A Change of Art
Conscious Decisions
Surrounded by Mercy
Broken Bonds
Mercy's Healing
To Heal a Heart

A Cross to Bear
Merciful Secrecy
Sunken Hopes
Hair Today, Gone Tomorrow
Pain Relief
Redeemed by Mercy
A Genius Solution
A Hard Pill to Swallow
Ill at Ease
'Twas the Clue Before Christmas

Find more inspiring stories in these best-loved Guideposts fiction series!

Mysteries of Lancaster County

Follow the Classen sisters as they unravel clues and uncover hidden secrets in Mysteries of Lancaster County. As you get to know these women and their friends, you'll see how God brings each of them together for a fresh start in life.

Secrets of Wayfarers Inn

Retired schoolteachers find themselves owners of an old warehouse-turned-inn that is filled with hidden passages, buried secrets, and stunning surprises that will set them on a course to puzzling mysteries from the Underground Railroad.

Tearoom Mysteries Series

Mix one stately Victorian home, a charming lakeside town in Maine, and two adventurous cousins with a passion for tea and hospitality. Add a large scoop of intriguing mystery, and sprinkle generously with faith, family, and friends, and you have the recipe for Tearoom Mysteries.

Ordinary Women of the Bible

Richly imagined stories—based on facts from the Bible—have all the plot twists and suspense of a great mystery, while bringing you fascinating insights on what it was like to be a woman living in the ancient world.

To learn more about these books, visit Guideposts.org/Shop